Corinna–Rosa Falkenberg

BECOMING ME:
THE ART OF TRANSFORMATION

AF287783

BECOMING ME:
THE ART OF TRANSFORMATION

Guided writing, drawing, and body-based exercises
created by Corinna-Rosa Falkenberg –
designed to spark creativity, nurture inner growth,
and perhaps even lead to transformation.

This books belongs to

_____

After the release of the short story collection 'Crazy for Life: In Love with Life' by Corinna-Rosa Falkenberg in 2020, the novella 'Don't kill me, I'm in love' followed in 2021. In 2022, the novel 'Pink Dolphins' and in 2023 the poetry book 'The sky and the salt' was published. All works have been translated into English and narrated as audiobooks by the author herself.
For more information about the author, please refer to the end of the book or visit www.corinna-rosa.com.

Corinna–Rosa Falkenberg

BECOMING ME:
THE ART OF
TRANSFORMATION

Illustrations by the author

BECOMING ME: THE ART OF TRANSFORMATION is a guide for those ready to engage with the full spectrum of their inner world—both the rational and the emotional, the analytical and the intuitive.

In a world that often overvalues logic and productivity, we are encouraged to live from the head up. Yet many of life's most meaningful decisions—and its deepest moments—cannot be solved with logic alone. This book brings the Thinker and the Feeler into dialogue: the two inner forces that shape how we navigate the world.

Through over 70 carefully designed reflections and exercises, you'll explore how to balance mental clarity with emotional presence. From managing stress and overcoming anxiety to processing grief and reconnecting with your body —each page invites you to train both your inner compass and your emotional resilience.

Created by Corinna-Rosa Falkenberg, whose personal story includes navigating early-life adversity and societal expectations, this book introduces the Phoenix Process: a practical framework for transformation that honors both intellect and emotion. Trained as an international lawyer with a doctorate in law, Falkenberg spent decades in the world of investment banking and international M&A project management—operating at the core of high-performance, logic-driven environments. Yet over time, she came to realize that logic, while powerful, has its limits. Today, under the name Artista Coco, she merges analytical clarity with emotional insight, inviting others to reconnect with the creative, intuitive side of themselves—the part that feels, senses, and transforms.

Each practice helps you explore yourself from both sides of the mind. The goal is not perfection, but wholeness: to feel at home in your thoughts and in your feelings.

WHO IS THE BOOK FOR?

This book is designed for those who seek to:

♡ **Emotional intelligence**
The ability to understand and lead yourself and others. A key competency for leadership and team dynamics.

♡ **Stress management and burnout prevention**
Effective self-regulation and early warning systems, crucial in high-performance environments.

♡ **Mental clarity in complex decision-making**
Integrating logic (The Thinker) with intuition (The Feeler) strengthens decision-making under uncertainty.

♡ **Inner resilience**
Building stability and health in the face of pressure, setbacks, and constant change.

♡ **Cognitive flexibility and innovation**
Accessing the right brain unlocks creative thinking, perspective shifts, and solution-oriented strategies.

♡ **Authentic leadership**
Leading not just with numbers, but with presence, empathy, and self-awareness.

♡ **Work–life integration**
Balancing personal and professional roles not through separation, but through conscious connection.

♡ **Sleep and energy management**
Sustainable performance requires more than discipline—it depends on the balance between body, emotion, and thought.

With grounding writing and drawing exercises, guided meditations, movement, and other activating techniques, BECOMING ME is more than a journey of self-discovery.

It is a training ground for emotional intelligence and mental clarity—so you can rise, fully and freely, as the person you truly are.

You don't need any prior experience—no background in art, poetry, athletics, or even self-reflection is required.
All you need is a curious, open heart and a strong willingness to embrace change.

Within these pages, I've carefully and lovingly gathered thoughts, impulses, and exercises that have been meaningful and effective for me on my own path.
My hope is that, by the time you finish this book, you will feel a deeper sense of clarity and positivity—and be empowered to sustain a high level of energy that allows your inner Feeler to grow and shine.

Enjoy the journey—and ride its waves.

With warmth,
Corinna-Rosa Falkenberg

TRANSFORMATION

"What the caterpillar calls the end of the world,
the master calls a butterfly."
– Laozi –

Transformation is the profound shift that touches the very core of who we are, reshaping us on a personal, emotional, mental, or even physical level. It's not just about making a few surface-level changes; it's about completely rewiring the way we think, feel, and act.

I experienced this firsthand when I went through a breakup in my mid-twenties. At first, I was devastated, feeling as though everything I knew had fallen apart. It took every ounce of willpower to recover from this heartbreak. During this process, I fundamentally changed my beliefs and habits. It was then that I realized I could transform into someone stronger, more self-aware, and more in tune with my own needs and desires.

The pain became my first catalyst for growth, leading me toward a version of myself I hadn't yet imagined. Slowly, I began to find my way back to my heart. For the first time, my rational mind and emotional world—the Thinker and the Feeler—started to move in sync. The two halves of my brain began to cooperate, rather than compete. To make it clear again: this process wasn't instant—it was a gradual journey of self-discovery, integration, and trust.

But real transformation doesn't happen just once. Years later—this time not through heartbreak, but through a quiet inner knowing—I made a decision that would change everything again: I left a successful career in international M&A project management to become an artist. It wasn't a breakdown that triggered this change. It was a buildup—a growing sense that success without meaning felt empty. That a life ruled only by logic left no space for creativity, connection, and emotional truth.

Becoming an artist in my mid-forties wasn't about leaving something behind. It was about reclaiming something I had long silenced. This time, the Thinker didn't step aside—he stepped into partnership with the Feeler. And that's where true transformation began to take shape.

TWO PATHS OF TRANSFORMATION

Disruptive, life-changing events can often be drivers of profound transformation. These events come in different forms, but they all have the power to initiate deep change within us.

SUDDEN, LIFE-ALTERING EVENTS

Sudden, life-altering events, such as the loss of a loved one, a major career change, or a personal crisis, can push us into a space where transformation is not just desired but necessary. These moments often force us to confront our vulnerabilities, question long-held beliefs, and reevaluate our priorities. While these changes are often painful, they can become the starting point for a new and more authentic way of living.

I have come to believe that it is in these moments of uncertainty and challenge that we are most open to deep, transformative change. When our old ways of coping no longer serve us, we are pushed to find new ways to navigate the world. Though it might feel like we are walking in the dark, every small step forward can illuminate a new path. It's during these periods of upheaval that transformation is most profound.

GRADUAL, SELF-INITIATED GROWTH

On the other hand, transformation doesn't always stem from dramatic, external events. It can also arise from a slow, intentional process of self-reflection and inner work. In fact, some of the most lasting changes occur when we consciously choose to evolve, setting aside time for introspection, learning, and self-improvement.

Whether it's through meditation, journaling, therapy, or simply becoming more mindful in our daily lives, gradual growth allows us to transform in a way that feels sustainable.

It empowers us to make changes not because we are forced to, but because we want to align more closely with our true selves.

For me, this kind of transformation has been just as important as those triggered by external events. Over the years, I've developed habits and practices that continuously guide me toward becoming the person I aspire to be.

These small, daily shifts have had a cumulative effect, leading to profound changes over time.

I now see transformation as a lifelong journey—one that evolves as we do.

PHASES OF TRANSFORMATION

The process of transformation is a deeply personal journey, one that I've come to understand through my own experiences. It often begins with a life-changing event or a moment of clarity—an awareness that something in your life must change. For me, I was heartbroken after being left, feeling completely lost and unsure of how to move forward. Climbing out of that emotional "rabbit hole" seemed impossible at the time.

The next step was letting go, which is often the hardest part. I had to confront the fears and doubts that were holding me back and release the old habits and beliefs that kept me stuck in place. This was a time of introspection, where I had to get honest with myself about what I thought was possible. It wasn't easy, but it was necessary.

Once I began to let go, I started exploring new possibilities. I tried out different paths, learned new skills, and opened myself up to opportunities I never would have considered before. This was a phase of experimentation and discovery, where I allowed myself to invite new ideas and ways of being into my life.

Finally, there came a point when these changes started to feel natural. The new insights and behaviors that once felt so foreign to me became a part of who I am. I integrated these shifts into my daily life, and they began to define my new normal.

Transformation takes incredible courage and patience. When I was going through my own period of change, I found myself relying on deep self-reflection and the unwavering support of friends and mentors. It wasn't just about altering my relationships or tweaking the external aspects of my life; it was about digging deep and experiencing profound inner growth. aspects of my life; it was about digging deep and experiencing profound inner growth.

This journey forced me to confront parts of myself I had long ignored. As I peeled back the layers, I began to understand who I really am—not just who I thought I should be. It was a process of becoming more confident, more authentic, and more in tune with my true self.

Now, when I look back on that time, I realize that transformation isn't just about making changes in how we think or act—it's about shifting our entire perspective on life. It's about seeing the world, and ourselves, in a new light. And while the journey was anything but easy, it ultimately led me to a place where I feel stronger, more genuine, and ready to welcome all the potential that life has to offer.

My journey to falling in love with life has begun.

WHAT'S IN THE BOOK FOR YOU

INTRODUCTION

CHAPTER ONE: BURN TO ASHES

CHAPTER TWO: GROW YOUR WINGS

CHAPTER THREE: RISE, PHOENIX

CONCLUSION

WHAT NOW?

MORE

ABOUT THE AUTHOR
ACKNOWLEDGEMENTS
SPACE FOR YOUR IMAGE AND WORD

INTRODUCTION

POWER OF ACTIVATION

"Mindset ist everything."
– Wim Hof –

There's an undeniable power in self-discovery, a power that no one can take away from us. I am deeply passionate about crafting experiences through inspiration, ideas, and exercises that will become truly yours, whether you're just beginning your journey toward a richer life or looking to elevate your current path to new heights.

The key to feeling vibrant lies in what we nourish our bodies with, whether it's thoughts or food. We often forget that we humans are an integral part of nature.

My life has been full of challenges, and I've learned from the school of life. This is why I'm passionate about creating an avenue for those who are striving to establish an abundant, fun, and healthy lifestyle, gain leverage over health and mental issues, or find a deeper connection to themselves—because that's fundamentally a deeper connection to everything: the world around us, our colleagues, friends, and family. I love sharing ideas based on my experiences, the kind I wish someone had shared with me when I was younger, to make life a little less tough.

How does this lifestyle give us greater leverage and a deeper connection? It seems that everything is a 'vibration' or a 'frequency'. With the latest tech, we understand that now.

So if the thoughts we think give off these 'vibes' then what is driving these thoughts? One of the contributors is an activated body and mind. If you are activated, and are in a high-energy vibe, then what vibrations have you got running through you right now? Are they life force vibrations?

When we are activated, it's all about good vibrations—because that's what harmony truly is: a symphony of good vibrations. If we are in harmony with nature, then, according to natural law, we too will thrive, just like nature.

The subtle energy of your body influences your mind, and vice versa.

This energy shapes your environment, your presence, and ultimately your present and future.

A FEW WORDS ABOUT ENERGY

"Energy is contagious.
Either you affect people or you infect people."
– Anonymous –

Energy is the essence of our life. We are energy.

In the realm of existence, energy flows as our life force.

It is our energy force that shapes our reality.

As soon as we recognize the power of energy in our daily lives and learn to measure our own energy level state, new worlds open up for us.

Energy is the essence that drives our actions, thoughts, and emotions, connecting us to our environment and to each other. By harnessing, cultivating, and activating our energy, new worlds might unfold right in front of us. Our energy level determines whether we can achieve balance, harmony, and vitality in our being.

Like a river that ebbs and flows, energy must be allowed to move freely within us without resistance or blockages. It's worth considering the importance of letting energy circulate within your body as often as possible.

How you can activate this state of being is the key aim of my book. Through practices shown in this book, you will be enabled to tap into the infinite source of energy that surrounds us and of which you are made.

"Qi", the Japanese refer to as "Ki", the Hindus describe as "Prana", the Greeks knew as "Pneuma", the Egyptians called "Ka", the Native Americans understood as "Great Spirit", and the ancient Celts recognized as »Anam".

Maybe you want to start practicing to honor energy as a sacred gift. This might help you to regularly check in on your own energy levels.

Kindly be reminded: Energy flows, as does your energy state. It may change in the next second and will never remain the same.

Within this understanding lies a tremendous opportunity:

the past is the past,
and in every moment,
you can co-create a new version of yourself with life.

Life is energy.
We are life.

                                   the princess
                              stands on the rooftop
                                   of the castle
                                     one night.

and jumps.

          she jumps into the dark nothingness.

                    it surprises her that she can fly,
                 that she doesn't need wings for it.

why the princess didn't take off yesterday,
didn't dare to,
she can no longer explain today.

From THE SKY AND THE SALT, page 105.

WHY FREEWRITING CAN HELP

"Start before you're ready."
– Steven Pressfield –

A large part of the exercises in my book consist of writing exercises. It's important for you to understand that writing in this context does not mean writing a scientific text, nor a novel, a speech, or a poem. The aforementioned writing styles are not addressed here.

What we are looking for is a creative exercise that is called 'freewriting'. This means that you write continuously for a set period without worrying about grammar, spelling, or structure. The goal of freewriting is to unleash your thoughts and ideas without inhibition and judgment, allowing your creativity to flow freely.

During freewriting, you write whatever comes to mind, without pausing to edit or censor yourself. The most important thing is to write without stopping. That is the key.

When I don't know what to write, I write exactly this down:

"I'm forced to write something but I f*ing don't know what to write right now. This exercise is terrible, I don't feel comfortable. What should I do...«

Yes, I write things like this just to keep my flow going. It usually takes only a few sentences like this, and then I get past the block, and the words start coming on their own.

This technique is often used to overcome writer's block, generate new ideas, or explore your subconscious state of being.

Freewriting can be done on any topic, from personal experiences to fictional stories and even on business plans. It is one of the most valuable tools for brainstorming and problem-solving for me.

By letting go of perfectionism and self-judgment, freewriting encourages your spontaneity.

You will see that you're able to foster a deeper connection with your Feeler—that intuitive, emotional part of you that responds before the mind begins to analyze.

And your Feeler is your source of energy.

When you're in touch with it, you're alive, honest, and fully present.

As with every art in life, also freewriting needs practice. I strongly encourage you to trust the process and stick to the exercise. As it is mostly done with a timer behind (at least that's how I do it), you know that time is limited.

THOUGHTS ON THE OTHER EXERCISES

Other than the writing exercises, this book includes physical exercises such as specific poses and hand gestures, as well as meditation ideas, breathwork, and drawing suggestions. There's no need to be an athlete, a yogi, or an artist. All exercises are suitable for beginners.

Here are some tips to ensure we're all on the same page:

1. All the writing exercises are freewriting exercises. Please do your best to 'just' write down the first thought that comes to your mind. Don't judge, don't censor. My idea behind this training is that you **lose control and delve into your subconsciousness**. Be reminded that what you write does not need to make sense at all, and you do not need to show it to anybody afterwards.

2. The **'Phoenix Process' consists of three stages**, which are also reflected in the chapters of my book: 'Burn to Ashes,' 'Grow Your Wings,' and 'Rise, Phoenix' Each stage represents a key part of the transformation journey—letting go of old patterns, embracing new growth, and ultimately rising renewed. I would say it's best to go through the exercises page by page, but hey, who am I to say this? Feel free to do as you feel—trust your own flow and intuition.

3. For many of the exercises, I've included prompts designed to spark your creativity. Some prompts are questions, while others may simply invite you to observe. Either way, they serve as an **invitation to begin your own expression.**

4. Sometimes, I have included bodywork exercises. Please don't skip them, but give the best you can. In particular, the breathwork will help your nervous system relax, so that your mind and heart can open up to get closer to

your inner life force. I will label your inner creative source sometimes your ‚Feeler', 'inner teacher' or simply 'life force'. **Please keep in mind that those are just labels. Feel free to call them however you want to call them.**

5. The first chapter, ‚burn to ashes', is maybe the most challenging one as there are many traumas included. Take breaks if needed.

6. **Stay present.** This is the golden rule because it doesn't matter if the pose is perfect when your mind is taking you away to the past or the future. The only right time is NOW.

7. If you breathe, let your breath be louder than your thoughts to reach the essence. Avoid fire breath exercises when you are carrying a child in your womb.

8. When the paper in the book is not sufficient, get yourself a journal or just some random extra paper.

9. Search the edge but don't push yourself too much. I call it **'discipline with softness'** or 'try and do the best you can'. You own your body, so you know what's best for it. Let go if an exercise is not right for you at that very moment. It can change in the next second, so feel free to come back to it. And if it still doesn't feel right in your body, just skip it.

10. Be aware that **some effects of the exercises appear only afterwards**, so observe yourself with an open mind.

11. Remember, in this process, **there is no right or wrong.** Each experience is personal and unique to you, and how you respond to the exercises will vary from moment to moment. It's important to release any expectation of 'doing it perfectly' or getting it 'right.' **This journey is about exploring yourself without judgment, embracing whatever arises without labeling it as good or bad.**

Trust that whatever you encounter—whether it feels profound or confusing—is exactly what is meant to surface at that time.

Give yourself permission to simply be, knowing that the only goal is to stay present and open to the experience.

HOW I STARTED
CONNECTING TO MY FEELER

I grew up in an environment where mothers wished their daughters were invisible. Within my family it's preferred to silently endure and complain about the neighbors rather than change things.

I had a childhood where at the age of 9, I had already undergone four heavy surgeries, each lasting for hours. My insides were cut open, worked on, and stitched back together.

Almost 40 years later, friends describe me as an "energetic bundle," while enemies might call me a "workhorse" due to my relentless dedication to drawing, writing, working, and accumulating academic titles and other qualifications.

All of that: liberation blows. It was my way of finding myself.

Sure, I often drive those around me crazy with it. But what remains in every phase: I break free from the conventions of my upbringing and become more myself with each passing day. I cannot do it any differently than I do now.

I could also not have become the person I am without my creative expression. Already in early school, I eagerly wrote in my daily diary, kept my sketchbooks and pen with me all day, and even painted with lipstick in the absence of art supplies. Now, as an adult, I have a part of my art studio in my van to keep it mobile.

I started to write and do art by simply doing it, forgiving myself when an art piece was not as I intended. My strong will to not give up helped me.

"Find something
that you are passionate about,
keep it,
and work on it every day."

Whether those are the exact words or who originally said them, I can't say for sure.

But does it really matter if they resonate with you?

you were born with the strength to fall,
so why not also with the power to rise again.

– let your wings grow.

From THE SKY AND THE SALT, page 259.

WHY THE FEELER IS OF IMPORTANCE

"Art is the signature of civilizations."
– Beverly Sills –

The Feeler is the breath of humanity, the language of our emotions—like air, wind, water, and fire. It senses our sorrows, smiles, sights, and the click of a camera shutter capturing moments in time. It holds both the cry and the humor of life.

You feel through your Feeler when you fall in love for the first time, when you embrace life with passion. And it is also your Feeler that breaks when your heart does. It reaches out between two individuals before they unite, and it stays with you as you take your final breath, crossing into the unknown. It permeates your daily existence like a refreshing bath—for those who dare to feel.

The Feeler awakens when you rise from the depths of grief, when you bask in the scent of summer, or when you lose yourself in the night sky. It pulses in moments of intimacy, flickers in the curiosity of a loved one's gaze, and weaves itself into the fabric of your personal myth. Surviving the trials of everyday life while staying open to feeling is an art in itself. Your life is a masterpiece—crafted by the quiet courage of your Feeler. And in the end, expressing that is not about perfection, but presence: dancing in the rain, painting after a loved one's departure, or penning poetry amidst life's mess.

**To live through the Feeler
is to be fully, wildly, vulnerably alive.**

I'M CREATIVE

"Creativity is intelligence having fun."
– Albert Einstein –

I become sad when someone says, "I am not creative."

Somehow, we have convinced large parts of humanity that they lack creativity. But this is not true. Creativity is not a gift reserved for a selected few; it is an inherent trait within each of us.

Creativity is our inner creator, guiding us from the very beginning of our journey. We have simply forgotten how to recognize, communicate with, and harness it. It is present with us, right beside you as you read these lines.

And just like creativity, your Feeler lives within you.
It, too, has been with you all along—quiet, subtle, often overlooked. But it is the very part of you that senses when creativity stirs. It is your Feeler that responds when beauty moves you, when color excites you, when a sentence gives you goosebumps. To reconnect with your creativity is to reconnect with your Feeler—to listen more deeply, feel more fully, and trust what arises from within.

As human beings, we are inherently imaginative. Our imagination has been crucial for our survival over millennia, constantly helping us devise new solutions to challenges.

As children, we were naturally curious and engaged with the world around us. We scribbled and drew, invented our own languages, and imagined beings that others insisted were just figments of our imagination. Our innocence and sense of freedom fueled our creative expression and our eagerness to explore the unknown, even if it meant taking risks. Observing children—a delightful way to spend your time—reveals how fully they live in the present moment. They don't dwell on the past or worry about the future.

Somehow, we lost those qualities on our way to adulthood.

We drew less, learned to write in standardized forms, and to speak in a common language our environment understands.

We were put into kindergarten; some of us had additional classes to attend, such as ballet class or piano lessons. Our responsibilities grew with the homework we received from school, so we didn't have a lot of energy left for other things. And suddenly, we were adults with even more responsibilities to carry.

Given this development, it's no surprise that many people feel unsure about using a pencil and paper, often saying, "I can't do this; I'm not creative." What they may actually be expressing is: "I'm too afraid to try because I doubt my abilities and worry that others will laugh at me if the result doesn't turn out well."

One fundamental aspect of being human is our desire to belong to a community and our fear of losing that sense of belonging if we are ostracized.

Yet, we all carry within us an inner child—the part of us that yearns to experiment, explore, and take risks. This inner child not only reminds us of the joys of life but also holds the wounds from our past and childhood, seeking transformation through love.

Nurturing this inner child allows it to come out and play joyfully, helping us reconnect with a more vibrant and authentic self.

Creativity is more than painting, drawing, or writing.

Creativity is cooking lunch, finding excuses why you can't come to Christmas, organizing bills, leading a professional discussion, working as a project manager, learning a new skill, finding different ways to say "I LOVE YOU" to your environment, falling in love with the flaws in life, listening to your child or pet and organizing a weekend getaway with loved ones.

All of this is creativity.

Creativity also manifests in problem-solving at work, crafting a thoughtful gift, designing a garden, rearranging furniture to refresh your living space, creating a budget, inventing a new family tradition, or even devising a plan to stay motivated during challenging times. t's evident in how you adapt to changes, overcome obstacles, and find beauty in the mundane. All of this is creativity.

It is our life force, a vibrant thread of our energy that connects everything we do and experience.

burn to ashes,
grow your wings,
rise, phoenix.

CHAPTER ONE:
BURN TO ASHES

1. TRAUMA

"Trauma is personal. It does not disappear if it is not validated.
When it is ignored or invalidated the silent screams continue internally
heard only by the one held captive."
– Anonymous –

The following chapter is the most emotional one as it deals with trauma. Trauma often blocks or distorts the natural development of the Feeler, because in moments of overwhelm, the system learns to shut down sensitivity in order to survive.

My youth was marked by verbal, emotional, and physical abuse. As a young girl, I was surrounded by a family that preferred to mask their true emotions and instead engaged in conflicts over trivial matters. We never developed problem-solving skills; we did not communicate or strive for positive change. I was never taught how to be vulnerable but was instead conditioned to become a warrior.

To survive, I learned to suppress my feelings, to stay alert, to calculate, to control. I was trained to rely on my Thinker— the part of me that analyzes, anticipates, and intellectualizes everything. And while the Thinker helped me navigate danger, it also disconnected me from my Feeler—from softness, intuition, and trust.

To cope with the harsh reality of my hometown, I turned to pens, canvases, and paper, creating a new reality of my own. Through this creative expression, I began to connect with my Feeler—and to discover parts of myself I never knew were there.

Do I have trauma from my upbringing?
    –Sure.
Do I pity it?
    –No, but it took me until my 40th birthday to reach this point of view.

Trauma helps you to grow, to expand, to go into the unknown, to activate you. It fine-tunes your character. And yes—you can either let the pain of trauma drag you down, or you can choose to upgrade your life because of the experience.

This choice is yours alone.

I decided to upgrade.

BELIEVING
SOMETHING
CAN
MAKE
IT
HAPPEN.

2. DEFINITION OF TRAUMA

"The greatest freedom is the freedom of choice.
When we reclaim our ability to choose, we reclaim our power."
– Anonymous –

Trauma can be defined as a loss of choice.

We did not have the option to protect ourselves, stand up for ourselves, maintain boundaries, or uphold our values.

This loss can feel profoundly extreme—so much so that we may not even be aware of our ability to choose in any given moment.

Our autonomy becomes obscured by survival patterns and ingrained programming.

We seek safety in individuals who ultimately cannot provide it, longing for validation that aligns with a persona that isn't truly reflective of who we are.

We find ourselves on paths that do not belong to us, but rather ones we feel compelled to follow because of past experiences.

All of this stems from a pivotal moment in which our ability to exercise autonomy was taken away.

Coming back to your own energy source—feeling activated —requires the restoration of choice and the reclaiming of autonomy. It involves making decisions about when and how we feel safe, establishing and maintaining boundaries, and charting our own paths forward.

It also means giving ourselves the time and space to gain clarity on what we truly desire and who we really are.

This process may involve discomfort as we become accustomed to making our own choices.

It takes time, but it is possible.

OBSERVE
IT
TROUGH
A TELESCOPE.
TURN
THE TELESCOPE
AROUND.

3. YOUR ENERGY LEVEL

– Required time: 10 min –
--You need: a quiet spot, pen & timer –

1. Allocate 10 minutes for yourself. Find a peaceful spot—it could be your favorite place at home, a creative corner in your office, or a serene spot in nature. Put the timer to 10 minutes, start now.

2. I encourage you to sit down, close your eyes, and connect with the earth. Do you feel your weight resting on it? Can you sense how securely it supports you?

3. Breathe in and out three times, counting slowly to four with each breath in silence: 1-2-3-4 in, 1-2-3-4 out. Observe how your nervous system begins to calm down.

4. Open your eyes, and (re-)read my quote on the left page, take your time.

5. Now, take your pen and turn to the next two pages. Answer the following question by using a 1 to 10 scale: How would you rate your current energy level, with 1 being very low and 10 being very high? Write the number down.

6. Please use the remaining time to list possible reasons for your current sensations. Continue writing in a freewriting style until your timer signals the end of the 10 minutes.

7. Remember: There is no right or wrong—only your way of doing it.

♡

Set the timer for 10 minutes and start now: *Possible reasons for my current sensations are...*_____

_____

_____

_____

_____

_____

_____

_____

_____

_____

_____

_____

_____

_____

_____

_____

_____

_____

_____

_____

_____

_____

_____

4. FEEL

– Required time: 8 min –
– You need: just you –

1. Now I want you to reflect on the last exercise on page 53. Set your timer for 8 minutes. Give each question about 2 minutes of your time:

   1. **What thoughts came up?**
   2. **Where in your body did these thoughts manifest?**
   3. **If your emotional state had a color, what would it be?**

      Don't overthink it – go with your first impulse. Let the color reflect your mood or inner tone.

   4. **How do you feel now?**

2. Did you finish writing before the timer beeped?

3. If you managed to keep writing continuously throughout the full 10-minute session in the previous exercise, you can go straight to the next page. You're already familiar with the rare phenomenon I call 'flow momentum'.

4. For the rest of us, I kindly suggest (re-)reading pages 28f. on freewriting to get more comfortable with the process.

Friendly reminder:
Take it easy.
You will get there.

i could have been the woman of many men,
but i wanted to be only yours.

— crazy.

5. WHAT DOES YOUR TRAUMA LOOK LIKE?

– Required time: up to you –
– You need: pen, timer –

1. Please close your eyes and take 3 deep breaths in and out. Tune into yourself and meditate on the idea of 'trauma'.

2. Then silently answer the following two questions in your mind:

   • **What does trauma mean to you?**
   • **What was your first experience with trauma?**

3. I invite you to take a pen and draw what your current trauma looks like in your mind.

Here are some steps to guide you through your drawing:

FIND A QUIET SPACE

Choose a calm, quiet place where you can focus without interruptions.

RELAX AND REFLECT

Take a few deep breaths and allow yourself to relax. Close your eyes if it helps, and reflect on your feelings and experiences.

VISUALIZE YOUR TRAUMA

Think about the emotions, images, or symbols that represent your trauma. It might be an abstract shape, a scene, or a combination of colors and lines.

START DRAWING

Begin to put your visualization on paper. Don't worry about artistic skill—focus on expressing your feelings and thoughts.

USE COLOR IF NEEDED

If you feel the need to use colors, go ahead. Different colors might help you express different emotions or aspects of your trauma.

USE THE NEXT TWO PAGES FOR YOUR DRAWING.

Remember, this exercise is for you and you alone.
Take your time and be as expressive as you need to be.

Don't overthink it–just start!

1. Draw what your current trauma looks like:

2. Now, look at your drawing and write down your first observations—without judgment—in a few words or sentences.

_____

_____

_____

_____

_____

_____

_____

_____

_____

_____

_____

_____

_____

3. Without thinking, just pick out 3 words from your text above, randomly.

1._____

2._____

3._____

4. You will now write three paragraphs in freewriting style, using one of the words from above in each paragraph. Each paragraph should include one of the chosen words, maintaining the chronological order.

To facilitate the energetic flow of creativity, please start from the sentence **'The sunny side of a fraction is...'** and complete the phrase.

First paragraph with first word:

The sunny side of a fraction is... _____

_____

_____

_____

_____

_____

_____

_____

_____

_____

_____

_____

_____

Second paragraph with second word:

The sunny side of a fraction is... _____

_____

_____

_____

_____

_____

_____

_____

_____

_____

_____

_____

_____

Third paragraph with third word:

*The sunny side of a fraction is...*_____

_____

_____

_____

_____

_____

_____

_____

_____

_____

_____

_____

5. Draw how you feel right now.

Remember, there's no right or wrong. Your drawing can be as simple as a single line or color, or as complex as you like. It could be a line, a flower, a raindrop—whatever resonates with your current state. Let your pen follow your mood.

6. POWER BREATHING

– Required time: 10 minutes –
– You need: your breath, timer –

Deep rhythmical breathwork for 30-40 cycles. Count to a 4/4 beat: in 2, 3, 4 and out, 2, 3, 4.

Breathing deeply from your belly, chest, and then into your head. The exhalation should have no force, just let go and relax.

Creating an ocean-like sound while breathing can help make your breath smoother. You can use your hands to guide your breathing; be creative, as there is (again) no wrong or right way to do it.

This type of breathing supercharges your body with vital oxygen, and you may feel a tingling sensation as if a current of energy is passing through you.

🖋 **Breathhold after final exhalation:** Hold your breath for as long as it feels comfortable, allowing your body to relax into a deep meditative state. Use this time to channel the energy from deep breathing or to focus on an intention. This practice floods your cells with oxygen, dilates blood vessels, and opens new capillaries, ensuring a fresh supply of blood to your organs, particularly your brain.

🖋 **Breathhold after final inhalation:** When you can no longer hold your breath, take a deep inhalation, filling your belly, chest, and head with air. Then hold your breath for 20 seconds, or as long as comfortable. This practice enhances oxygenation, promotes relaxation, and helps to balance your nervous system. It also encourages a sense of calm and focus, improving overall mental clarity and physical well-being.

This is 1 round. Begin a new round and repeat for a total of 4 rounds.

Do this in the morning to supercharge your mind and body for the day ahead.

Do not do this in water or while driving, as you will likely get hurt, and I don't want that.

Enjoy!

♡

7. LETTER WRITING

– Required time: 30 minutes –
– You need: pen, timer, and optionally, a fireplace –

In moments of feeling blocked or uninspired, I find solace in revisiting the exercise of writing a letter.

I maintain a list of prompts that I'm happy to share with you. I always select the one that resonates most with me at that particular moment.

These prompts offer a sense of comfort, as they focus on ideas that are familiar and meaningful to me—concepts I've pondered extensively, though I may still be searching for solutions (at least for now).

Typically, I set aside 30 minutes to write these letters.

Once completed, I often burn them in the fireplace by my door. I find joy in releasing the energy and setting its spirit free. Reusing the same prompt multiple times doesn't bother me, as I always uncover new thoughts and insights each time.

Set the timer for 30 minutes, choose one of the following prompts, and start your freewriting.

You can always redo the exercise and choose another prompt.

☼ **Write a letter to your future self, reflecting on where you hope to be in five years.**

☼ **Address a letter to a future generation, sharing your hopes and aspirations for the world they will inherit.**

☼ **Pen a letter to a younger version of yourself, offering advice and encouragement.**

☼ Write a letter to a loved one who has passed away, expressing things you wish you had said.

☼ Address a letter to someone who has deeply impacted your life, sharing your gratitude and memories.

☼ Write a letter to a fictional character, discussing how they've influenced your thoughts or actions.

☼ Craft a letter to someone you admire but have never met, explaining why they inspire you.

☼ Address a letter to a place that holds special meaning for you, describing your memories and emotions.

☼ Write a letter to your inner critic, challenging its negative beliefs and affirming your worth.

☼ Pen a letter to your fears, acknowledging their presence and committing to overcome them.

*Dear...*_____

_____

_____

_____

_____

_____

_____

_____

_____

_____

8. CAT & DOG

– Required time: 10 min –
– You need: mat or cushions, pen, timer –

1. Make sure you have a mat or cushions.

2. **Kindly go on your knees and hands.** Lengthen your neck.

3. **Breathe in and out** while silently counting to four in a steady rhythm.

4. When you are ready, **exhale and make a cat back by bowing upwards.** Count again to four as you breathe in.

5. Then **breathe out while slowly lifting your face toward the ceiling or sky,** and your back arches downward. Breathe out to a count of four.

6. I suggest you repeat this ten times.

7. This exercise is a lovely evening activation as it calms the nervous system. Closing your eyes during the exercise will make it even more intense.

8. Once done, sit on your heels with your eyes closed and simply observe.

9. When it feels right, take your pen and write down the sensations you just experienced on the next page.

Describe your sensations:

_____

_____

_____

_____

_____

_____

_____

_____

_____

_____

_____

_____

_____

_____

_____

_____

_____

_____

_____

_____

_____

9. WHO AM I?

– Required time: 20 minutes –
– You need: pen, timer –

Take some minutes and observe the drawing.

If the drawing could speak,
what would it tell you about yourself?

Set a timer for 20 minutes and start writing continuously until the time is up. Don't stop—this is key—even if it means you end up writing nonsense.

_____

_____

_____

_____

_____

_____

_____

_____

_____

_____

_____

_____

_____

_____

_____

_____

_____

_____

_____

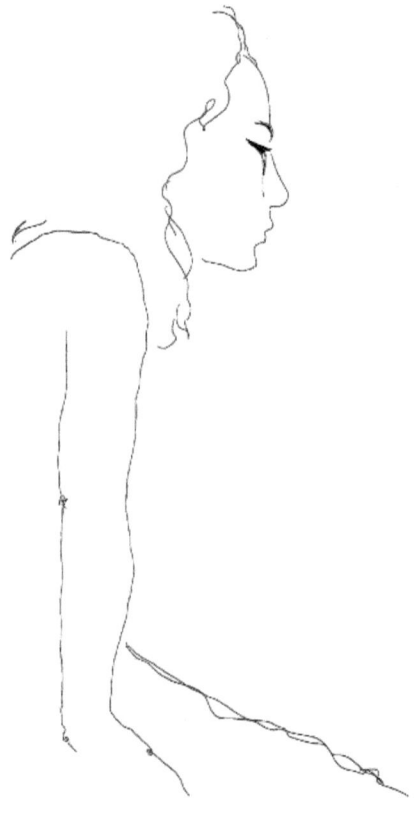

HOW
HONEST
DO YOU (I)
WANT TO
LIVE?

why has no one ever told me
how much it hurts?
why can i find nothing written about it,
nowhere something sung?
why does sorrow strike me
right in the core of my being—
then, when the best friend leaves without reason?

no warning,
no quarrel,
no open conflicts.
the process insidious,
unreachable once.
i thought nothing of it at first.
but by the second time,
it felt peculiar.

in concern, i called for a third time;
her husband, curtly, said:
"sorry, she has no time."

excuse me?
until now, we could always hear each other,
even at the most impossible hours.
everything was possible for both of us.
we licked the remnants off the same pudding spoon,
giggled at jokes only we understood,
discussed the unspeakable.

tell me, what has changed for you,
what did i do wrong,
what is wrong with me?

say something, please—anything!
but stop ignoring me!
we've been through a lot,
laughed tears, cried tears.
what's going on, what have i done to you?

i can't find peace,
seek you out,
darken my eyes,
want to know why, how?
but you only say:
go, it's over.

i beat my fists against it,
but it does nothing.
you say nothing more.
and when i don't stop crying,
your husband sends me away,
wordlessly, his finger pointing to the courtyard.

separation grief usually refers to romantic love,
but why has no one ever told me
that it hurts just as much,
when the best friend leaves?

From THE SKY AND THE SALT, page 26f.

10. FRIENDSHIP

– Required time: up to you, usually 15 minutes –
—You need: pen, timer –

This writing exercise consists of two parts.

Part One: **Describe the situation when a friendship ended. How did it happen? How did you feel at that moment and in the aftermath?**

Part Two: **Reflect on and describe the views, ideas, and actions that helped you overcome the heartache from the end of that friendship.**

First part: _____

_____

_____

_____

_____

_____

_____

_____

_____

_____

_____

_____

_____

_____

Second part: _____

_____

_____

_____

_____

_____

_____

_____

_____

_____

_____

_____

_____

_____

_____

_____

_____

_____

_____

_____

_____

_____

_____

_____

_____

_____

_____

_____

_____

_____

_____

_____

_____

_____

Once you have reached this point, **please summarize the strengths mentioned above in the second part that helped you;** these are your resources for resilience.

Write them down as five bullets:

• _____

_____

• _____

_____

• _____

_____

• _____

_____

• _____

_____

11. CHOCOLATE MEDITATION

– Required time: up to you –
– You need: pen, your favorite chocolate –

1. Find a comfortable place where you won't be disturbed.

2. **Take a piece of chocolate and place it in your hand.** Notice its shape, texture, and temperature. Is it beginning to soften in your palm? How does it feel—smooth, firm, slightly yielding?

3. **Observe the weight of the chocolate.** Is it heavier or lighter than expected? Turn it slowly in your fingers and notice its surface—ridges, imperfections, shine.

4. **Pause and notice your own desire.** How much do you want to taste it? Where in your body do you feel that anticipation—your mouth, your stomach, your fingertips?

5. Bring the chocolate **close to your nose and inhale deeply.** What do you notice—sweetness, earthiness? Had you ever paid attention to its scent before?

6. **At half your usual speed, or even slower, bring the chocolate to your lips.** Let your lips touch it gently before taking it into your mouth.

7. **Place it on your tongue without chewing.** Close your eyes. Let it sit. Let your tongue rest. Don't move.

8. **Observe how the taste begins to unfold.** What do you feel first—sweetness, depth, warmth?

9. **Keep the chocolate in your mouth as long as possible.** Notice your shifting desire—do you want more, or are you already satisfied?

10. When the chocolate has dissolved, **take a deep breath.** Feel your mouth, your body, your presence. This moment of attention is a gift. Receive it fully.

Try to **eat consciously and mindfully** for the rest of the day. Approach each meal with the same sense of awareness and enjoyment that you experienced with the chocolate.

Take note of which flavor felt the most bland to you:

Which element had the most distinct or intense flavor?

Which element exceeded your usual expectations in flavor or enjoyment?

Which experience felt the most unusual or unexpected?

12. GAINING STRENGTHS
FROM OBSTACLES

– Required time: up to you –
– You need: pen –

Read the following prompt, and freewrite your thoughts:

List other challenges you've overcome in the past. For each, describe how the experience contributed to your personal strength, resilience, or self-understanding.

*It happened...*_____

_____

_____

_____

_____

_____

_____

_____

_____

_____

_____

_____

_____

_____

_____

_____

13. CAT & DOG WITH FIREBREATH

– Required time: 10 min –
– You need: mat or cushions, pen, timer –

Kindly redo the exercise on page 72 with the following differences:

1. **Use the fire breath:** Fire breath is a powerful pranayama technique that involves rapid and forceful exhalations through the nose, often practiced in yoga to generate heat and energy in the body. To do the fire breath technique, take quick, forceful breaths through your nose, making a sound like 'ha.'

2. **At the same time you exhale the rapid breath, bow your back upwards, while you bow it downwards when you breathe rapidly in.** The movements are very quick, so you might need a bit of time to figure out the technique. That's part of our journey, so go for it.

3. No need to count, **do the exercise for 60s** – and maybe another round for 180s.

4. While you breathe in and out rapidly, focus on the sensation of heat and energy in your body.

5. Be reminded to do this exercise with caution, as a lot of energy will flow into your body. **Listen to your inner teacher** and stop the exercise once its purpose is fulfilled for you.

6. This exercise is an amazing morning activation. When you close your eyes during the practice, it may become even more intense. If this practice doesn't feel right for you, gently return to the exercise on page 72—without judging yourself.

7. Once you feel the time is over, sit back on your heels with your eyes closed and simply observe.

8. When the moment feels right, take your pen and write down the sensations you experienced on the next page.
Then, compare the outcome between the exercise on page 64 and this one:

1. To what extent do they feel different?
2. What happened to your energy level?

Give each practice a score between 1–10.

Write down the sensations you experienced during this practice:_____

_____

_____

_____

_____

_____

_____

_____

_____

_____

_____

_____

_____

_____

_____

_____

_____

_____

_____

_____

_____

_____

_____

_____

_____

TO CEE
OR
NOT TO
SEE ?

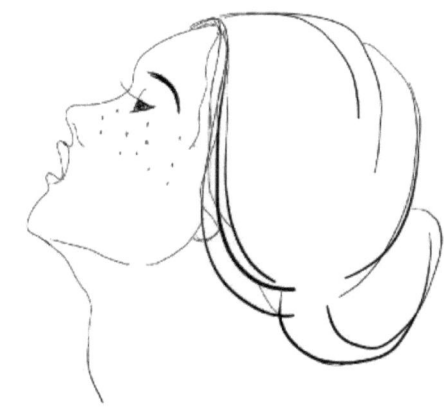

14. FAVORITE PLACE

– Required time: up to you –
– You need: pen –

Feeling comfortable in life also means knowing the places where you can reconnect your left and right brain — and gently recharge your energy. Take a moment to read the prompt and freely write down your thoughts:

Describe your favorite place and why it means so much to you.

My favorite places is . . . _____

_____

_____

_____

_____

_____

_____

_____

_____

_____

_____

_____

_____

_____

_____

_____

_____

_____

_____

_____

_____

_____

_____

_____

Now write down how you can make more time to spend at your favorite place in the future:

_____

_____

_____

_____

_____

_____

_____

_____

_____

_____

_____

the strongest, most compassionate people
i've had the privilege to encounter
have walked over the hot coals
of their inner wounds.

they chose
not to be burned by them,
but to turn the heat into medicine.

15. WRITE DOWN ONE MESSAGE YOU WILL <u>NEVER</u> SEND:

WRITE DOWN ONE MESSAGE <u>YOU WILL SEND</u> TODAY:

16. YOUR MEDECINE

– Required time: 15 minutes –
– You need: pen, timer –

Re-read my poem on page 98 and **reflect on the idea of turning wounds into medicine.**

Without overthinking, **name five of your inner wounds and how you transformed them into transformation.** Let each wound show you the hidden gift it carried all along. Summarize your 'medicine' with one word. This word can be a color, a fruit, an animal, or a deity. Let this word become a symbol—a quiet reminder of your inner strength and capacity to grow. You can return to it whenever you forget how far you've already come.

1

INNER WOUND	TRANSFORMATION	NAME

	INNER WOUND	TRANSFORMATION	NAME
2			
3			

	INNER WOUND	TRANSFORMATION	NAME
4			
5			

17. SUNSHINE

– Required time: up to you –
– You need: just you in nature –

Enhance your morning routine by **waking up just 20 minutes earlier than usual**. As soon as you rise—and without overthinking—gently **head outside for a short walk within the first hour of waking**. This small shift can create powerful momentum for the rest of your day.

If the sun is out, take a moment to face it with closed eyes. Simply breathe and allow yourself to feel. **Let the light touch your skin**, your eyelids, your presence.
If the sun isn't yet visible, consider using a **sun lamp** with at least 10,000 lux—it can be just as effective in helping your body awaken gently and naturally.

Sunlight triggers the production of **serotonin**, often called the happiness hormone. It uplifts your mood and helps regulate your body's natural rhythm between day and night. This is not just science—it's a practice of alignment.

Over time, I've noticed how this ritual brings more clarity, steadiness, and energy into my day. And to be honest: my dog Bobbino plays a big part in keeping me consistent. His joy in early morning walks reminds me daily that movement and light are gifts we can receive if we simply say yes to the day.

Later on, you may feel inspired to design your own unique morning ritual by combining elements from this book. There's no one-size-fits-all—only what resonates with you.

Take your time. Stay curious.

18. SHADOW WORK

– Required time: up to you –
– You need: just you in nature –

I find the term 'shadow work' quite meaningful, as it emphasizes the **courage and effort it takes to confront the darker aspects of ourselves**—those that follow us silently, like our own shadow.

Engaging in shadow work means delving into the deepest recesses of our inner world and learning to meet what we find there with **acceptance**. It often involves facing unresolved issues rooted in our relationships with our parents and other aspects of our past, so that we may stop projecting them onto past, present, or future partners.

Only by consistently turning toward our shadows can we cultivate **authentic self-awareness**—and from that place, build genuine connections with others.

I remember being afraid at first. Facing my inner demons felt overwhelming, unfamiliar, and uncomfortable. It took time to become familiar with them. But the years I spent doing this work have proven worthwhile.
As I got to know my shadows better, **their power over me slowly diminished**.

Today, I even enjoy drawing them. Sometimes, they still look frightening—other times, I can laugh at how absurd they seem. They will always be close to me, like a shadow—but over the years, I've learned how to live with them.

And perhaps more importantly, how to lead them rather than be led by them.

Describe your inner demons: Are there more than one? What do your inner monsters look like—and how do they show up in your life? How do they shape your thoughts, influence your feelings, or direct your actions?

Do you believe your inner demons are changeable? If yes, how might you begin to transform them?
What practices or strategies help you face them, soothe them, or even befriend them?

And finally: **What does it feel like to acknowledge and confront your inner monsters?** What shifts when you allow yourself to meet them, rather than avoid them?

Set a timer for 10 minutes.

Let your pen guide you—without judgment, without needing to fix anything. Just be present with what is.

*My inner demons look like…*_____

_____

_____

_____

_____

_____

_____

_____

_____

_____

_____

_____

_____

_____

Draw your inner monster(s):

Maybe you just want to relax after that last deep dive?

Be my guest.

You've earned a moment to breathe, stretch, or stare at the sky for a bit.

THE ENEMY
IS FEAR.
WE THINK
IT IS HATE
BUT IT
IS REALLY
FEAR.

-EMPOWERED-

19. ADMIRATION

– Required time: 45 minutes –
– You need: pen, timer –

Over time, I've come to appreciate the value of having a diverse and nourishing circle of people around me.

Ideally, this circle includes: one-third of people to whom I can offer support and energy, one-third with whom the relationship feels mutual and balanced, and one-third who embody qualities I deeply admire—qualities I wish to invite more of into my own life.

Now it's your turn to reflect.

Think of three people in your life—friends, acquaintances, or even colleagues.

For each of them, write down: the life challenges they've faced (as far as you know), what you admire about how they've handled them, and which of their inner strengths or qualities you'd like to cultivate more within yourself.

Take your time. Be honest. Let this be an exercise in gratitude, empathy, and gentle self-growth.

First person/ Name: _____

Challenges the person had to face: _____

_____

_____

_____

_____

_____

_____

_____

_____

_____

_____

_____

_____

_____

_____

_____

Why do you admire this person, and which of their inner strengths or qualities would you like to cultivate more within yourself?: _____

_____

_____

_____

_____

_____

_____

_____

_____

_____

_____

<u>Second person/ Name:</u> _____

Challenges the person had to face: _____

_____

_____

_____

_____

_____

_____

_____

_____

_____

_____

_____

_____

_____

Why do you admire this person, and which of their inner strengths or qualities would you like to cultivate more within yourself?: _____

_____

_____

_____

_____

_____

_____

Third person/ Name: _____

Challenges the person had to face: _____

_____

_____

_____

_____

_____

_____

_____

_____

_____

_____

_____

_____

_____

Why do you admire this person, and which of their inner strengths or qualities would you like to cultivate more within yourself?: _____

_____

_____

_____

_____

_____

_____

20. LET GO OF PEOPLE

– Required time: as much as you need –
– You need: pen –

Another lesson I had to learn the hard way is to **let go of people who are not ready to love you**.

This is one of the hardest things you'll ever have to do in your life, and it will also be one of the most important.

Let go of showing up for people who are not interested in your presence, as it **steals your time, energy, mental, and physical health.**

When you decide to live a life filled with personal development, joy, positivity, interest, and commitment, not everyone will be ready to follow you to that place.

That doesn't mean you have to change who you are; it means you have to let go of people who aren't ready to be with you.

If you are excluded, forgotten, or ignored by the people you dedicate your time to, you are not doing yourself a favor by continuing to offer them your energy.

The most valuable things you have in your life are your time and energy—both are limited.

The people and things you give your time and energy to will define your existence. Make your life a container where only people 'compatible' with you are allowed in your inner circle.

You need to do this to protect your energy.

Think about someone in your life **whom you need to let go of**, whether due to a change in circumstances, personal growth, or unhealthy dynamics.

Write a letter to this person, expressing your feelings, memories, and the reasons why it's time to move on. This time, I invite you to use a separate sheet of paper to write this letter (not in this book).

This letter is just for you. **It will not be sent.** It's a space for your truth — a gentle release, not a confrontation.

Focus on acknowledging the impact they had on your life, expressing gratitude for the good times, and explaining why letting go is necessary for your well-being.

After writing the letter, reflect on how this exercise helps you come to terms with the decision to let go.

Once finished, and once you feel ready, burn the written words in a ceremony of your choice. Maybe you want to do it during a full moon, in the morning hours, or on a Sunday. Maybe you feel the need to be surrounded by loved ones (your spouse, closest friend, or your dog), or you need to be alone.

Whatever it is, do it.

21. CONCERN

– Required time: 10 minutes –
– You need: pencil –

Write your biggest current concern in this box.

And now, imagine, your best friend is having this concern. What advice would you give him.

Write it down it the box above.

22. FEAR

– Required time: big exercise, as much as you need –
– You need: pen –

A dialogue from Momo to Master Hora:
"Are you Death?"
"If people knew what Death truly is, they would no longer fear it.
And if they no longer feared it,
then no one could steal their lifetimes from them."
"Then you just have to tell them."
"I tell them with every hour I allot to them.
But I think they prefer to believe those who instill fear in them."
– From Momo

During the last exercise, you may have noticed **how limiting worries can be.** How often do we hold ourselves back, fearing the opinions of others, and settle for a life that looks good on the outside but doesn't feel fulfilling on the inside?

The truth is, y**ou owe no one—especially not your parents—an explanation for your own path.** You are always allowed to change your mind and pursue entirely new directions.

Give yourself permission to follow your path, even if it isn't immediately understood by others, and acknowledge that you may face judgment along the way.

Make a list of six things you are the most afraid of:
(feel free to add your concern from the last exercise)

1. _____

_____

_____

2. _____

_____

_____

3._____

_____

_____

4._____

_____

_____

5. _____

_____

_____

6. _____

_____

_____

No one will ever walk in your shoes; you know yourself best, and you have every right to say, "Forget it, I'm doing this now," and to live your life not out of fear, but out of love for yourself.

Trust yourself. Trust the gentle voice within that guides you. Trust your abilities and the knowing that a loving force will always be by your side.

And believe this: In the end, everything will be okay. And if it's not okay yet, then it's not the end.

Now, take your pen and circle the top three fears out of the six listed on the last page. If you're having trouble deciding, close your eyes and pick one at random.

Let's explore these three fears together. For each fear, answer the following four questions: Where does it come from? What is it related to? How does it affect my life? Is it a rational fear, supported by facts that prove that the fear can become reality?

FEAR ONE:

Where does it come from?_____

_____

_____

What is it relating to? _____

_____

_____

_____

_____

How does it affect my life?_____

_____

_____

Is it a rational fear?_____

_____

_____

FEAR TWO:

Where does it come from? _____

_____

_____

What is it relating to? _____

_____

_____

How does it affect my life?_____

_____

_____

Is it a rational fear?_____

_____

_____

FEAR THREE:

Where does it come from? _____

_____

_____

_____

_____

What is it relating to? _____

_____

_____

How does it affect my life?_____

_____

_____

Is it a rational fear?_____

_____

_____

♡

Many people live out of fear. Many human relationships are even built on fear. Sometimes, this fear is so overwhelming that it casts a shadow over an entire life like a dark cloud. Then words slip from our mouths that we wouldn't otherwise say—words fear makes us speak. We do things we never intended to do, but fear drives us to them.

Out of fear, humans may have even carved gods from stone and begun to worship them—without ever having seen them in reality.

No one finds this idiotic, crazy, or insane. Why? Because everyone does it, just in different ways: one has a temple to go to, another a mosque, church, or synagogue.

But at its core, it's always the same: the prayers are filled with fear.

Like the fear of what comes after death, or the fear of what will happen if we don't live according to religion.

But there is only one way—and fear doesn't simply show it to you: it is the **way inward**.

The inward path seems like an effort only at the beginning. But soon you'll realize how playful and easy it becomes there. Gratitude arises. And perhaps even your own personal inner heaven.

And in that place, there is no room for fear. Fear simply does not exist there. Fear needs society, friends, family, the state, religion. But inside you, there is only you. There you are alone—and that is not enough for fear. That's why fear always turns outward. It goes after reputation, money, power, God, death. It lives outside.

Don't even try to befriend fear. It doesn't need that. You only have to see it—then it disappears all by itself.

And be reminded that fears don't make us weak; on the contrary, they **make us human**. I have learned to distinguish two kinds of fears: **rational and irrational**. Irrational fears are based on feelings rather than facts.

For example, imagine I have a test the next day. The fear is irrational if—let's assume—I am well prepared and have never failed a test before. There is no real reason to expect failure tomorrow. Still, my fear is real, even though the probability that I will pass is much higher.

Whenever I ignored these irrational fears, I had the impression they grew stronger.

My experience with fears is that whenever I confront them directly, they diminish. Sometimes it took multiple confrontations for them to fade away, but eventually, they all did once I began to face them.

Drawing from my career in business M&A, I learned the **importance of risk management**, which I then applied to my personal life: I began to contemplate best-, worst-, and realistic-case scenarios, and started writing letters to my fear.

Now, I invite you to do the same.

Each time you meet fear with clarity and honesty, your Feeler grows stronger. By staying present with discomfort instead of avoiding it, you learn to trust your inner signals— and reclaim your emotional intuition. Your Thinker helps you assess and plan, but true transformation begins when you also bring your Feeler into the process. When both are acknowledged—logic and emotion—you can navigate fear with grounded awareness and authentic courage.

Let's do it together:

FEAR ONE:

What is the worst outcome that can happen? _____

_____

_____

What is best possible outcome that can happen? _____

_____

_____

What is the most realistic outcome that can happen?_____

_____

_____

On a scale from 1-10, how realistic is:

- worst outcome:
- best outcome:
- realistic outcome:

Now, write a letter to your fear.

If the fear is irrational and very unlikely to happen, thank your fear for being there and gently explain that it is time to leave. Remember to be kind, as your fear is not your enemy but your friend. Fears play an important role in warning us, and it is our responsibility to evaluate the actual risk.

If the fear is rational and likely to happen, write to your fear that you take it seriously and explain how you will proactively manage the risk. Reassure your fear that, in the end, everything will be alright.

_____

_____

_____

_____

_____

_____

_____

_____

_____

_____

_____

_____

_____

_____

_____

_____

_____

_____

_____

_____

_____

_____

_____

_____

_____

_____

_____

_____

_____

_____

_____

_____

_____

_____

_____

_____

_____

_____

FEAR TWO:

What is the worst outcome that can happen? _____

_____

_____

What is best possible outcome that can happen? _____

_____

_____

What is the most realistic outcome that can happen?_____

_____

_____

On a scale from 1-10, how realistic is:

- worst outcome:
- best outcome:
- realistic outcome:

Letter to your fear: _____

_____

_____

_____

_____

_____

_____

_____

_____

_____

_____

FEAR THREE:

What is the worst outcome that can happen? _____

_____

_____

What is best possible outcome that can happen? _____

_____

_____

What is the most realistic outcome that can happen?_____

_____

_____

On a scale from 1-10, how realistic is:

- worst outcome:
- best outcome:
- realistic outcome:

Letter to your fear: _____

_____

_____

_____

_____

_____

_____

_____

_____

Well done!

The last exercise was a huge mountain.

Take a break.

Do something pleasurable for yourself.

the way i love myself
   teaches not only him
      how he can and should love me,
         but also my entire surroundings.

From THE SKY AND THE SALT, page 30

23. YOU AS AN EMOJI

– Required time: 5 min –
– You need: a quiet spot, pens, timer –

The last exercise in this chapter is designed to help you unlock yourself even more so that you feel comfortable. Remember, no one is judging you except yourself. So put your inner policeman away, take a deep breath, relax, and begin.

Draw yourself as an emoji:

Now draw the emoji you would like to be:

to-do list
— to rediscover oneself on a sad day:

- cry it out and dry your heart.
- find shelter under a heavy blanket.
- put on your favorite music and dance to it with closed eyes, alone and naked.
- lock yourself in the bathroom and scream loudly.
- under no circumstances make an important decision.
- repeat to yourself 20 times "this too shall pass" and pat your forehead with the three middle fingers in a 1-2-3 waltz rhythm.
- drink hot cocoa with cardamom and cinnamon, if necessary, several times a day.
- light a candle and blow it out with the thought "tomorrow is a new day".
- spray lavender scent on your pillow and carry it into your dreams.
- before that, kiss a few trees in the forest.

From THE SKY AND THE SALT, page 246

...by now, you have become more familiar with your two inner sides: the Thinker and the Feeler. To make it more tangible, let's meet the shapes and different facets of the Feeler:

INNER WISDOM

The Feeler is the wellspring of your deepest insights and intuitive wisdom. It helps you navigate challenging decisions and uncover meaningful answers that go beyond logic. It invites you to pause, listen inwardly, and trust what you sense rather than what you can prove.

GUIDANCE

The Feeler offers orientation from within. It helps you notice what truly matters, find direction in times of uncertainty, and stay connected to your inner values. This kind of guidance often appears quietly – through sensations, moods, or sudden clarity when the mind steps aside.

SELF-LOVE AND ACCEPTANCE

Your Feeler encourages you to treat yourself with care and kindness. It supports you in recognizing your strengths and approaching your imperfections with understanding. It reminds you that your worth is not tied to performance, but to presence and authenticity.

TRANFORMER

The Feeler assists you in processing emotional wounds and difficult experiences. It gently guides you toward self-care, emotional clarity, and inner balance. By allowing emotions to be felt rather than suppressed, it opens the door to genuine transformation and resilience.

CREATIVE INSPIRER

The Feeler inspires you to engage in creative activities and explore new possibilities. By connecting with this side, you unlock your artistic abilities and awaken your creative energy. It encourages you to follow your curiosity, take creative risks, and express yourself beyond words.

SOURCE OF GUIDANCE AND CLARITY

The Feeler offers direction and clarity during moments of confusion or uncertainty. It helps you define your goals and confidently follow a focused path. It does so not through fixed plans, but through subtle cues, inner resonance, and emotional alignment.

BRINGER OF PEACE

The Feeler helps you find inner peace by guiding you to slow down and reconnect with the present moment. It encourages you to notice what you feel, without needing to fix or analyze it.

By connecting with your Feeler, you can access a profound **reservoir of wisdom, strength, and emotional depth**. Can you feel it already?

The more you engage in dialogue with this inner presence —no matter whether it feels abstract or familiar—the more visible and palpable it becomes over time.

It takes time, so be patient.

CHAPTER TWO:
GROW YOUR WINGS

24. ACTION THROUGH WORDS

"We write to taste life twice, in the moment and in retrospect."
– Anaïs Nin –

I started writing because I wanted to keep exploring who I truly am. To follow the thread inward, deeper than I had ever dared to go. I began with a diary—simple, private, raw. It was the first place I allowed myself to tell the truth, even if I didn't yet understand it.

Drawing and painting brought me closer to my emotions, to my Feeler, but they couldn't help me untangle certain knots in my mind.

Writing did. It gave form to the formless. It turned fog into language. It let me walk around my thoughts, observe them, reshape them.

And so I kept writing —not to arrive at a final answer, but to stay in conversation with myself. Because the self is not a destination. It's a landscape. And writing is how I learn to navigate it.

Who am I without the context of my family—without the backdrop of a village nestled in the Bavarian Alps? I have been writing since the age of twelve. My words were always about liberation—about breaking free from the narrow confines of that village. I wrote about dreams. About hopes. About the vastness I sensed beyond the silhouettes of the mountains.

Over the years, my writing began to take new forms.
I created the *Cocoletters*—fragmented notations, moments, and reflections composed in a distinctive handwritten script. A script that winds its way through my paintings and drawings, sometimes hidden, sometimes boldly visible. Words not just written, but embedded—interwoven into color, texture, and form.

But over time, I grew weary of writing about where I could have been, what I could have done.

Eventually, I became so tired, I couldn't write at all.

That's when a voice within rose up and said:

> *"Your words are empty without action. Only you have the power to live your life. No one else."*

It was then that I finally understood the true force behind my writing: My words can inspire action—but it is up to me to live them.

Through the following exercises in this second chapter, I invite you to deepen your understanding of who you truly are—your core—independent of your environment.

Only when you become aware of yourself—your strengths, weaknesses, belief systems, and fears—can you begin to live the life you truly desire. And when you learn to befriend your Feeler, to accept its sensitivity rather than resist it, you gain access to a deep inner compass. Instead of being overwhelmed by emotion, you learn to move with it—to manage it with presence, not control. You become grounded, yet receptive. Vulnerable, yet powerful. No longer at the mercy of your inner tides—but surfing them with clarity and grace. Because only then will you have become your truest self.

Remember: this journey is lifelong. Learn to ride its waves.
Embrace the imperfections.

And strive to make the most of each wave that comes your way.

25. LOVE

– Required time: 15 minutes –
– You need: pen, timer –

When preparing to write, I often begin with mind maps.

I place the main subject in the center of the page and then, without overthinking, jot down every thought that comes to mind around that word.

I don't judge or censor myself—this exercise is simply a container for collecting ideas.

Now it's your turn:
On the next page, **write down everything that comes to mind when you think of love.**
Set a timer for 15 minutes—and keep writing without stopping until the time is up.

Let your associations run wild: Words, memories, colors, smells, quotes, people, places, feelings. Write down what love feels like in your body. What it once meant. What you long for, what scares you, what you've learned. There are no wrong answers—only raw material. Let the page hold all of it.

LOVE

if i may,
i would like to wish us to let our wings grow wide,
to dare to fly with them,
but at the same time never forget
how beautiful it is to stand firmly on the ground.

if i may,
i would like to wish us
to recognize our own weaknesses in each other
and to respond to them with compassion.

if i may,
i would like to wish us
to see nothing but love—in each other,
in our surroundings, and within ourselves.

and most importantly,
to have the courage to live that love.

From THE SKY AND THE SALT, the end

26. YOUR LOVE STORY

– Required time: up to you –
– You need: pen & a loving heart –

I invite you now to **write three love stories** you have experienced. For each prompt, pick the first one that comes to mind. **Be generous with positive words,** and feel free to use **joyful exaggeration** to more easily capture the essence.

Describe each situation as vividly and lovingly as possible. Then continue freewriting with the prompts I provide.

1. Write about your experiences with your parents. Describe a moment when you truly felt their love:

*It was without doubt that...*_____

_____

_____

_____

_____

_____

_____

_____

_____

_____

_____

_____

_____

_____

_____

_____

_____

_____

_____

_____

_____

_____

_____

_____

_____

_____

_____

_____

_____

_____

_____

_____

_____

_____

_____

_____

_____

_____

2. Write about your experience with a friend. Describe a moment when you truly felt their love.

*I felt happy when…*_____

_____

_____

_____

_____

_____

_____

_____

_____

_____

_____

_____

_____

_____

_____

_____

_____

_____

_____

_____

_____

_____

_____

_____

_____

_____

_____

_____

_____

_____

3. And now write about your experience with your girlfriend or boyfriend. When did you feel their love?

It was obvious that ..._____

_____

_____

_____

_____

_____

_____

_____

_____

_____

_____

_____

_____

_____

_____

27. SELFLOVE

Self-love is the foundation for loving animals, rivers, trees, and flowers. It's also the foundation **for falling in love with someone else**.

That's why I want you to love yourself more today than you did yesterday.

Place one hand on your heart and one on your belly.

Close your eyes.

Take three slow, deep breaths.

Now, gently bring this sentence into your mind—
"If I truly loved myself today, I would..."

Let the words echo in you.

Notice what thoughts, images, or feelings arise.

There's no need to force anything—just observe.

Let it be a quiet offering to yourself.

Then, when you're ready—
read the poems on the next pages.

the stars in the sky,
they claim,
that my home
is right in my heart.

they whisper that to me
whenever i feel lost.

— i am home within myself.

be gentle to yourself,
that too is love.

– self-love.

28. WHAT DO I LOVE ABOUT MYSELF?

– Required time: 30 minutes –
– You need: pen, timer –

I invite you to write down thirty characteristics, skills, and abilities that you absolutely adore about yourself. Don't hold back. In this exercise, I encourage you not only to use the most positive descriptions you can find but also to exaggerate a bit, as if you were talking about your best friend. Promise yourself that you won't take a break until you have finished all thirty.

I absolutely adore about myself…

1. _____

_____

2. _____

_____

3. _____

_____

4. _____

_____

5. _____

_____

6. _____

_____

7. _____

_____

8. _____

_____

9. _____

_____

10. _____

_____

11. _____

_____

12. _____

_____

13. _____

_____

14. _____

_____

15. _____

_____

_____

16. _____

_____

17. _____

_____

18. _____

_____

19. _____

_____

20. _____

_____

21. _____

_____

22. _____

_____

23. _____

_____

24. _____

_____

25. _____

_____

_____

26. _____

_____

27. _____

_____

28. _____

_____

29. _____

_____

30. _____

_____

Now kindly reread the list twice before you go to bed
tonight, and continue again the next day.

Feel.

≡

29. YOUR POWER ANIMAL

– Required time: 30 minutes –
– You need: pen, timer –

Now, with this fresh day, please **revisit the list you wrote on the last pages**. Go through each item, inhale, exhale, and once you've reviewed the entire list, I invite you to close your eyes and embark on a **journey of imagination**.

What is appearing in your mind right now? Do you see an animal? Maybe a large, wild creature—or perhaps something smaller and familiar? It might even be a mythical or entirely imagined being. Take a moment to observe it. What colors surround it? Are there scents, sounds, or textures in the air? Where is this creature—what kind of environment is it in? Is it moving? Still? Watching you? Allow the image to unfold without judgment. You don't need to analyze—just notice. Let your imagination lead the way.

Whatever it may be, hold onto this image and capture it in your mind's eye. If you lose sight of it, start again: review the list of 30 items, close your eyes, and see what emerges. It may only be present for a moment, so be ready to grasp it. Then move closer, observe, and if you feel inclined, engage with whatever has appeared. Feel free to converse.

Use the next page to sketch what you've seen. Don't worry about making it perfect—this isn't about artistic skill, but about giving form to your inner vision. **Let your hand move freely across the page**, following the shapes, textures, and emotions that emerged in your imagination. Feel free to use colored pens, pencils, or anything else you have on hand. Incorporate as many hues, layers, and details as you like. Maybe you focus on the creature itself—or perhaps you're more drawn to its surroundings, the atmosphere, the energy it carried. There's no right or wrong.

Placeholder for your drawing:

Once you're done, you might want to **take a picture** of your drawing with your phone. The artwork you've just created can serve as an **important reminder** if you ever lose your sense of self-worth. Whenever you feel weak, look at it, feel your strength, recognize your abilities, and remember how valuable you are to the world.

Enjoy!

30. WHAT SELFLOVE IS NOT

– Required time: 15 minutes –
– You need: pen, timer –

Now, write down what you believe self-love is NOT. Use the freewriting style. I will support you with the following prompt:

*Selflove is not when I'm...*_____

_____

_____

_____

_____

_____

_____

_____

_____

_____

_____

_____

_____

_____

_____

_____

_____

_____

_____

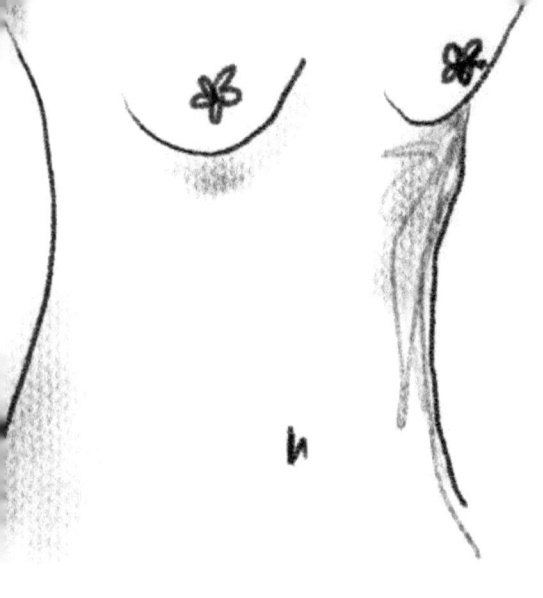

you say:
i love you,
but what you mean is:
i want sex with you.

31. TWO TYPES OF MEN

I wrote the following text years ago. It remains valid to me to this day. As a man, you might want to read it from your own perspective, as the text may be equally valid vice versa.

> In the realm of relationships, women often encounter two distinct types of men.
>
> The first type are those who seek growth and healing. Their wounds are visible, raw, and painful. These men are takers, often departing once they've exhausted what they can take from a woman.
>
> Then there's the grounded man, firmly rooted in his own life. He knows himself, and his desires are clear. This man has the capacity to provide the space a woman needs to tap into her own energy, reaching her higher self.
>
> In this partnership, energy flows on equal footing. No one feels drained; instead, both are invigorated.
>
> The last type of man is rare, but he does exist. It's up to us women to decide which type of man we welcome into our lives.
>
> The choice is yours.

32. FEMININE AND MASCULINE ENERGY

– Required time: 10 minutes –
– You need: your voice –

Engage the right side of your brain—the intuitive, emotional, and imaginative part of you.
Activate your *Feeler*, the area that senses rather than analyzes, that connects rather than controls.

Read the text on the right page aloud several times— however many you choose. This is your life, and only you can decide how deeply you want to engage with it.
In this spirit, you also decide how much you want to take from this exercise.

The key is to read the text consciously, with full presence.
Give it your all. Let the words move through your body, not just your mind.

Celebrate your voice by playing with it: change the tone, the volume, the rhythm, the pronunciation.
Try it softly, then boldly. Whisper it to yourself, say it out loud to a tree, a stranger, a friend—or just into the mirror.

Let your voice become an instrument.
Let it surprise you.
And as you speak, simply observe:
What shifts inside you? What do you feel?

This is not about performance. It's about presence.

Enjoy!

celebrating the power
of the feminine and the masculine today.

may all listen
to their intuition and their mind,
may all know
that the balance between heart and head
is key in life,
may all dance
together and create magic,
may all spread their light.

as one is nothing without the other,
as no gender is better than the other,
as each of us carries a wound,
as love is the only healing power.

33. THE WILD ANIMAL WITHIN

– Required time: 5 minutes –
– You need: courage & your most favorite dance song –

The untamed spirits within you are alive and vibrant. To awaken these primal forces, **immerse yourself in your favorite dance track**—the faster and more dynamic, the better.

Crank the **volume up to the maximum**, or, if you dare, **slip on your headphones and venture into a public space**. Dance with uninhibited fervor, as if each movement breathes new life into your soul. If possible, dance barefoot —feel the earth beneath you. If it feels right, shed even more layers. Skin against air. Body in freedom. **Let your body remember what it means to belong to itself.**

Listen closely to the whispers of your inner voice.

How do the primal beings within wish to manifest today? Perhaps they long to prowl the ground like a jaguar, stride with majestic grace like an elephant, or soar through the air like a bird.

This is not about finding a "power animal" or a fixed symbol. It's about tuning into the raw, instinctive energy that wants to move through you—right now.

Embrace the creature that first emerges in your mind's eye. Extend an invitation to dance, allowing the rhythm to guide your primal essence.

In this sacred moment, **let go of all inhibitions and dance as though the world fades away,** leaving only you and the pulsating beat.

Surrender to the primal energy coursing through your veins, for in this dance, you are truly free.

This final exercise is for the pros. It took me years to express myself authentically through my body, and dancing in front of others is still sometimes a challenge for me.

You might want to start by dancing at home, in your room, where no one—neither your children, partner, mother, nor friends—can see you. Use headphones for the music and try to express yourself with your eyes closed.

Treat this exercise as practice. **The key is to do it repeatedly and not give up.**

I needed my second home, Bali, to find that freedom. It was there that I experienced Ecstatic Dance in all its forms— wild, raw, silent, sweaty, tearful, sacred.

Those dances taught me that my body knows more than my mind. That I don't have to perform—I just have to show up. That movement can be prayer, release, rebellion, and joy— all at once.

So wherever you are, begin where you are.
You don't need a temple, just a song.
Let the dance become your teacher.

34. FRIENDLY REMINDER

Kindly be reminded that you will never sacrifice your strength for your softness, nor your softness for your strength.

Embody both energies as you swing between both frequencies.

35. CHANGED THINKING OR BEHAVIOR

– Required time: up to you –
– You need: pen –

Read the prompt, and freewrite your thoughts.

Describe a pivotal moment in your life that transformed your thinking or behavior. Use all three pages to explore it fully.

_____

_____

_____

_____

_____

_____

_____

_____

_____

_____

_____

_____

_____

_____

_____

_____

_____

36. SCULPTURE STYLE

Growing up in an environment where women were expected to remain silent, words became invaluable to me. During my legal studies, I honed my language skills, learning to articulate situations in detail and construct persuasive arguments. While I often revel in playing with words and expressing myself generously, there are moments when I recognize the power of brevity—a few carefully chosen words can have the exact impact I desire.

Through poetry writing, I've come to appreciate the allure of concise, impactful phrases. They not only convey deep meaning but also bring a sense of calm to my mind by distilling complex situations into key expressions. This process reminds me of my experience with wood sculpture, where I remove unnecessary pieces to reveal the desired form.

It's important to note that not all thoughts or content lend themselves to this style. However, embracing brevity has helped me clarify my thinking and decide when to use each approach.

Here are further examples of the sculpture style for you:

the red ladybug on my arm,
its tickle on my skin.

i look at him,
i hear his warm voice—
it wants to tell me about you.

but i flick him away.

you were a queen
who could fly
before he came,
and
you will be a queen
who can fly
after he's gone.

37. SACRED WORDS

– Required time: up to you –
– You need: pen & timer –

This exercise consists of two parts, in which you will write your own sculpture poem. I will guide you through the entire process.

Remember: don't overthink, just have fun!

Begin writing at length about a time when you truly felt loved.

Set a timer for 10 minutes and begin: _____

_____

_____

_____

_____

_____

_____

_____

_____

_____

_____

_____

_____

_____

_____

_____

_____

_____

_____

_____

_____

_____

_____

_____

_____

_____

_____

_____

_____

_____

_____

_____

_____

_____

_____

_____

_____

_____

_____

_____

_____

Now, you will revise the piece you have written. First, re-read your text and write down its two key messages. **How would you summarize it for a friend?**

_____

_____

_____

_____

_____

_____

_____

_____

_____

With your key messages in mind, reread your text and **remove any sentences or words that don't directly support your main points**. Be generous with your edits. Once you're clear about the lines you want to keep, write them down here:

_____

_____

_____

_____

_____

_____

_____

_____

_____

Thirdly, grab some extra sheets of paper and condense what you wrote into six lines. This is an intensive process and may take some time, so remain patient!

As you edit, refer back to your two key messages to keep your communication clear. Embrace the process and be satisfied with the best version you can create for this exercise. Perfection isn't necessary—focus on the journey.

Remember, you can revisit your poem in the future and continue shaping it in the weeks and months ahead!

Once you feel ready for now, **write down your final six lines here**:

_____

_____

_____

_____

_____

_____

Now, look at your six lines and **shorten them further**, while making sure they still support your key message.

_____

_____

_____

_____

_____

_____

_____

38. MAKING AN IMPACT

– Required time: up to you –
– You need: pen –

How can you make a positive impact on the world?

Have you ever pondered this question? For most of my life, I hadn't. It wasn't until I was traveling in India that I was asked this question for the first time—and it has stayed with me ever since.

How can I make a positive impact on the world?

This question has become important to me because it prompts me to consider contributing to something beyond myself, something greater than me. I also believe that this helps to balance self-love.

Without looking beyond one's inner self, love cannot be balanced. True balance arises when self-love roots us—and love beyond the self lets us grow beyond our own edges.

Use the space provided below and on the next page to engage in freewriting, exploring how you can make a positive impact on the world. Read the prompt I've provided and start writing without overthinking.

*I am a gift to the world because I am...*_____

_____

_____

_____

_____

_____

_____

_____

when my mother carried me within her,
at a time when security and love
were the only things i knew of the world,
you were there too.

your cheeks pressed against her belly,
i heard your soft voice,
received your tender words.
—they were addressed to me.

it was the first declaration of love
a man ever made to me.

—fatherly love.

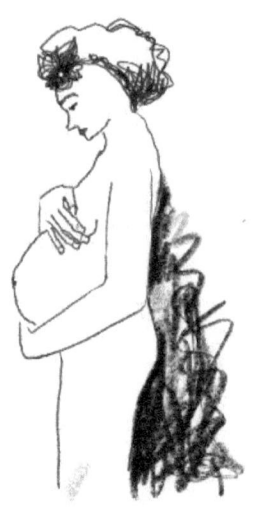

39. LETTER TO YOUR DAD

– Required time: up to you –
– You need: pen –

We often conceal our pain from those closest to us, because opening up can feel like exposing our vulnerability.

For this exercise, **I invite you to write a letter to your dad (or to the idea of your dad) and express any pain you feel related to him**. This doesn't have to be limited to pain he caused; it can include any hurt you have experienced throughout your life.

Read the prompt and start writing in a freewriting style.

*Dear Dad (or notion of Dad), I want you to know...*_____

_____

_____

_____

_____

_____

_____

_____

_____

_____

_____

_____

_____

_____

40. FOOD

There is a saying that nothing tastes as good as being healthy feels. One contributor to a fun, healthy lifestyle is food.

If food is a vibration, then what kind of vibrations would you like to consume? Life force vibrations?

Personally, I am a big fan of raw living food. Technically, when we heat food above 48°C (118°F), we begin to inactivate enzymes, and higher temperatures can lead to a complete loss of their activity. This also affects some nutrients; for instance, heat-sensitive vitamins like vitamin C can be significantly reduced.

Heating can alter the molecular structure of certain nutrients, potentially making them less bioavailable or effective for the body. Most importantly, from the perspective of Raw Living Food enthusiasts, this process reduces the "life force" within the plant, which is considered vital to its nutritional value.

Back home in Europe, I can't maintain this diet consistently, so I regularly take trips to Bali where I spend time eating only Raw Living Food. My experience is proof enough for me that my body benefits from this way of eating.

You are wise enough to make your own experiences.

Back home, I am 100% vegetarian and 99% vegan and love, love, love to make my food from scratch, always trying to chose local and organic ingredients free of additives whenever available.

I only fry in coconut oil and never use a microwave. I intentionally prepare and serve my food with love and good intentions.

I smile and have fun in my kitchen!

I believe that great meals serve not only as an expression of culinary creativity, health, and nourishment, but also as a platform for collaboration, community, and heartfelt communication.

In my own home, memories are built around sitting at the kitchen table, laughing with friends, and waiting for fresh bread to come out of the oven.

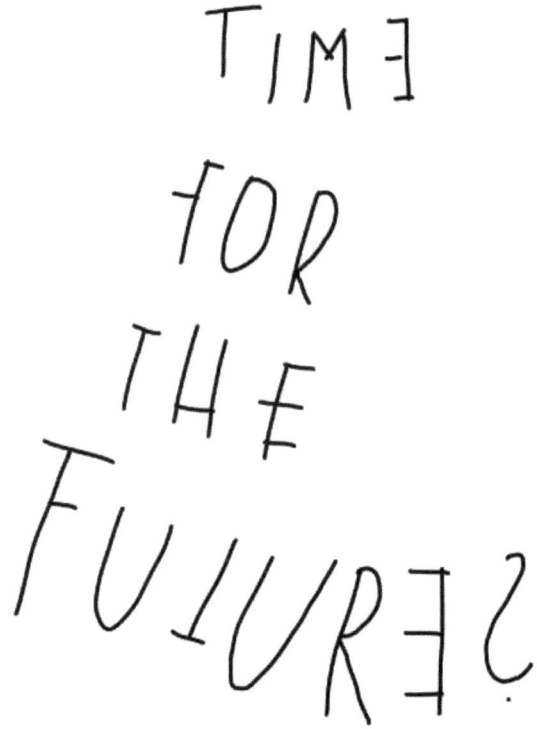

41. SLOW EATING

– Required time: up to you –
– You need: pen –

Next time you have a meal, take your time. Really take your time—so that you can chew, bite by bite. And if you're feeling courageous, try chewing each bite 54 times.

Observe. Feel. Taste.

Notice how the flavors unfold, deepen, and shift—from bold to subtle, from distinct to blended.

How do you feel when you take that much time to chew just one bite? What feelings begin to surface? Patience? Restlessness? Curiosity? Let them come. Just notice.

_____

_____

_____

_____

_____

_____

_____

_____

_____

_____

_____

_____

_____

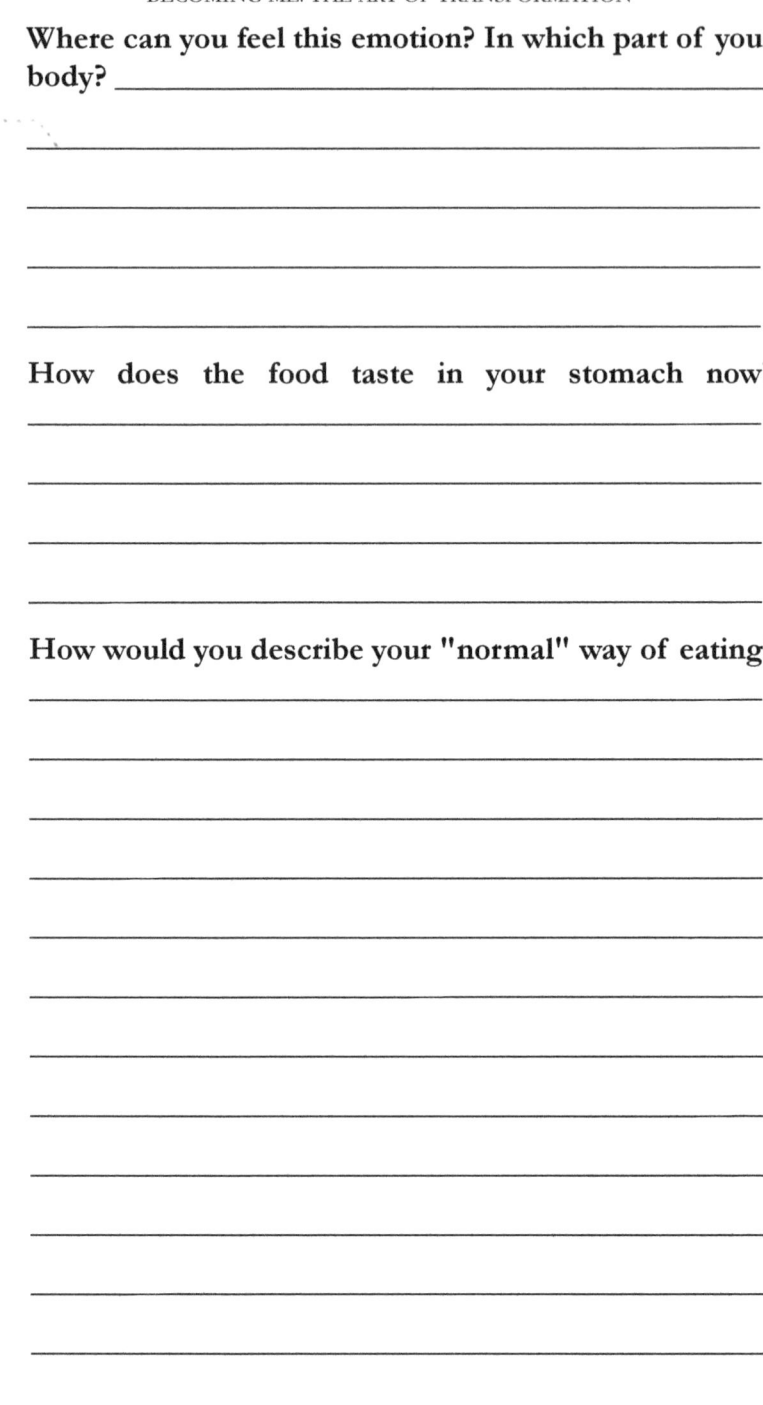

Where can you feel this emotion? In which part of your body? _____

_____

_____

_____

_____

How does the food taste in your stomach now?

_____

_____

_____

_____

How would you describe your "normal" way of eating?

_____

_____

_____

_____

_____

_____

_____

_____

_____

_____

_____

_____

in the act of love,
i often tried—sometimes to the point of despair—
to merge our separate ecstasies into a shared
transcendence.
searching for infinity:
without worries, without a yesterday, without a
tomorrow.
but in vain. even the last time, it eluded us.
        —exhausted, i collapsed onto you.

From THE SKY AND THE SALT, page 206

it takes all my courage
to relinquish control in the moment of orgasm—
to surrender to the animal within me.

—recognizing the animal within oneself, growth.

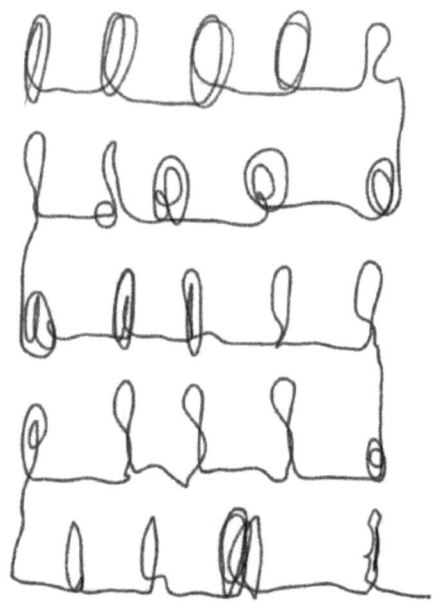

42. LETTER TO THE PERSON WHO FIRST TOUCHES MY BODY

– Required time: 20 minutes –
– You need: pen –

On the next pages, I gently invite you to write a letter to the person who first touched your body with a sensual or sexual intention.

Important: If this memory is painful or connected to a boundary that was crossed, please take a moment to check in with yourself. You are always in charge of your process.

If it feels too overwhelming, you might choose not to write this letter—or to write it from a place of protection, anger, grief, or distance.

You can also write to your younger self instead, or to someone you wish had been there for you.

Whatever you choose: your feelings are valid. Your story matters. This space is here to support you in reconnecting with your inner Feeler—that sensitive, intuitive part of you that knows, remembers, and responds. Not to retraumatize.

Be gentle with yourself. **Go only as far as feels safe.**

*To you who has touched my body...*_____

_____

_____

_____

_____

_____

_____

how could our love ever die
when i've already told
the stars, the sun, and the moon
about us?

43. THE TALK

– Required time: up to you –
– You need: pen –

Please read the prompt and continue writing in freewriting style:

If my yoni could speak, she would say... and if my phallus could speak, he would say..._____

_____

_____

_____

_____

_____

_____

_____

_____

_____

_____

_____

_____

_____

_____

_____

_____

_____

44. SEXUAL PLEASURE

– Required time: up to you –
– You need: pen –

Put your shame aside, read the prompt and continue writing in freewriting style:

I want you to touch my body like… _____

_____

_____

_____

_____

_____

_____

_____

_____

_____

_____

_____

_____

_____

_____

_____

_____

_____

_____

_____

_____

_____

_____

_____

_____

_____

_____

_____

_____

_____

_____

_____

_____

_____

_____

_____

_____

_____

_____

_____

_____

_____

_____

_____

45. SATURDAY NIGHT

– Required time: 30 minutes –
– You need: pen & timer –

Answer the following questions:

My favorite place is: _____

My favorite drink is: _____

My favorite talking topic is: _____

Now, using your answers, **write a narrative about a potential future experience** where you are in your favorite place, enjoying your favorite drink, while engaging in your favorite topic of conversation with a stranger you find very attractive. **You decide how the story ends.** Be aware that you are free to write whatever you wish. Your only limit is your imagination. Enjoy.

In the tranquil ambiance of... _____

_____

_____

_____

_____

_____

_____

_____

_____

_____

Re-read what you have written and examine your role:

To what extent have <u>you</u> created a flow between you and the other person? What did <u>you</u> do to co-create the dynamic with the stranger?

If you described yourself as more passive—which is perfectly fine—consider how you might have taken a more active role. Conversely, if you see yourself as more active—which is also perfectly fine—reflect on how you might have embraced a more passive role.

The goal is to create awareness of your conscious choices, allowing you to decide whether you want to be more active or more passive in a given moment.

Remember, you are the creator of your own life, and the decision is entirely yours.

Write down your thoughts in five bullet points, in a random order:

1. _____

_____

2. _____

_____

3. _____

_____

4. _____

_____

5. _____

_____

46. ASKING

– Required time: up to you –
– You need: pen –

We all have hidden dreams—wishes that require courage to speak out loud. There was a time when I kept my internal world to myself.

Over time, I learned that the more I practice voicing what I want, the more clarity I gain in life.

This also allows my counterpart to understand where I stand, enabling them to respond.

Speaking your truth is similar to freewriting; there is no editing involved. Trust me: the more often you try, the easier it gets.

Select one of the four situations and try to express your truth in your own words:

☼ **You want to get married, but you believe your partner hasn't been considering it. How would you express your inner desire to be heard?**

☼ **Your partner wants a baby, but you don't feel ready for it. How would you respond to them?**

☼ **You believe you deserve a promotion. As you meet with your boss for your annual review, what would you say?**

☼ **You feel like you've experienced a lot of burnout in your job over the past few months and years. You know that taking a sabbatical leave isn't yet common within your company. How would you approach your boss?**

Remember that you can always return to the exercise to complete the other scenarios.

Begin now: _____

_____

_____

_____

_____

_____

_____

_____

_____

_____

_____

_____

_____

_____

_____

_____

_____

_____

_____

_____

_____

it is just as important
to speak our inner truth
as it is
to say no.

47. THE POWER OF NO

– Required time: up to you –
– You need: pen –

Find a quiet place where you can reflect without distractions.

1. Take a few deep breaths to center yourself.

2. Think about a recent situation where you said "yes" but really wanted to say "no."

3. Use the next page to write down the situation in detail. How did it make you feel? What stopped you from saying no?

4. Now, imagine yourself saying a clear, kind, but firm "no" in that moment. Write down what you would say.

5. Reflect on how saying "no" could have changed the situation or your feelings about it.

6. Finally, write a short affirmation to remind yourself of the power and importance of saying no. For example: "I have the right to say no and honor my boundaries."

48. MY PERSONAL KEY RULES

Maintaining accountability to a set of rules I've developed to shape the life I desire has been invaluable to me.

Below is my current list—which is, naturally, subject to change as life evolves, and this adaptability serves me well:

1. ACTION

The nature of human existence is action. Through action, we provide and receive energy.

Ask yourself from which place you act, and make sure you choose the place of love. Become aware when you over-identify with your doing. Know that what you do can never complete you, as you are already complete as you are. Therefore, it cannot add anything to you, nor can it take anything away from you. Ask yourself: Am I acting from a place of love? If not, change your intention, your words, and your actions.

2. ADVENTURE

Adventure is always sparked by curiosity and the willingness to enter the unknown. It brings discovery, growth, and change to you.

Wow—that sounds like life? Yes! Life itself is an adventure! Throughout your journey in the world, every task you undertake is motivated by one of two things: love or fear. Fear always focuses on the outcome, believing that through accomplishment it will gain something. Love, instead, knows that the true treasures are revealed throughout the adventure itself!

3. ALLOWANCE

Allowance is the major key to complete freedom. To practice this art, first remind yourself that there are no mistakes in life, only experiences. Practice being fully present to every single experience you have—the good ones as well as the bad. Accept them all as they are. Be present with the things that disturb you, and balance your own disturbances by surrendering them to the stillness of your heart. In the end, you are like the wind: you can neither possess nor be possessed. Emotions come and go; they simply pass through you.

Trust the process!

4. AWARENESS

Awareness is a powerful dynamic of life itself. Awareness is forever innocent, as it is untrained by perceptions or beliefs. It does not accumulate thoughts or things of any kind. Practice viewing the world from this place. Look at things as though you have never seen them before, as if you were a child discovering the world around you, as if it is entirely new to you. Welcome all things, all movements, all connections, all emotions with great surprise and curiosity. By suspending the perceptual mind, you can experience a state of perfect peace and innocence. Thoughts, beliefs, and perceptions arise and pass away, but awareness remains!

5. BALANCE

The fundamental conflict in the world is between fear and love. You might believe that fear is beyond your control, but in truth, you've created it yourself. Fear often feels real—yet it may simply be the result of over-identifying with your Thinker. When you surrender to the heart, where the Feeler resides, fear begins to dissolve naturally.

Being aware of the mind's tendency to identify with passing thoughts provides a valuable opportunity to break free from the cycle of fear. When fearful thoughts arise, gently shift your awareness to the ever-present stillness of your heart and breath.

By surrendering these thoughts to your heart and breath, they naturally dissolve.

49. YOUR PERSONAL RULES OF LIFE

– Required time: loooong –
– You need: pen –

Create your own list. Consider this piece of writing as an experiment. Treating the things I do as experiments helps me simply start and take action. Remember, this list cannot be completed all at once; it's an ongoing project. Feel free to revisit it whenever it feels right. Add, delete, or clarify as needed. Everything is allowed. Appreciate the process, as it signifies your growth and development.

Begin by jotting down your personal rules for life:_____

_____

_____

_____

_____

_____

_____

_____

_____

_____

_____

_____

_____

50. CONGRATS

Congratulations to you! You've completed another chapter, delving deep within yourself and embracing the challenge to push your limits. This is a beautiful step forward.

Remember that you have the power to control how you perceive and discuss your challenges. Although they may seem burdensome, you can train yourself to view them as opportunities for growth and upliftment.

For me, maturity involves learning to navigate the waves of our emotions. Emotions will always exist, but we can train our minds to conquer our inner struggles rather than succumb to them. For me, maturity means learning to manage the Feeler—the part of us that senses deeply, reacts emotionally, and often resists logic. Emotions will always exist, but we can cultivate an inner sense of safety, even while feeling intensely. It's not about suppressing emotion, but about holding it—consciously.

This creates a healthy balance between the right and left hemispheres of the brain: between intuition and reason, feeling and thinking, chaos and clarity.

Construct your own reality in your mind, as external circumstances hold no sway over us whatsoever.

RISE, PHOENIX

there is only one journey
that truly matters in life,
and that is the journey
into our innermost self.

– the departure.

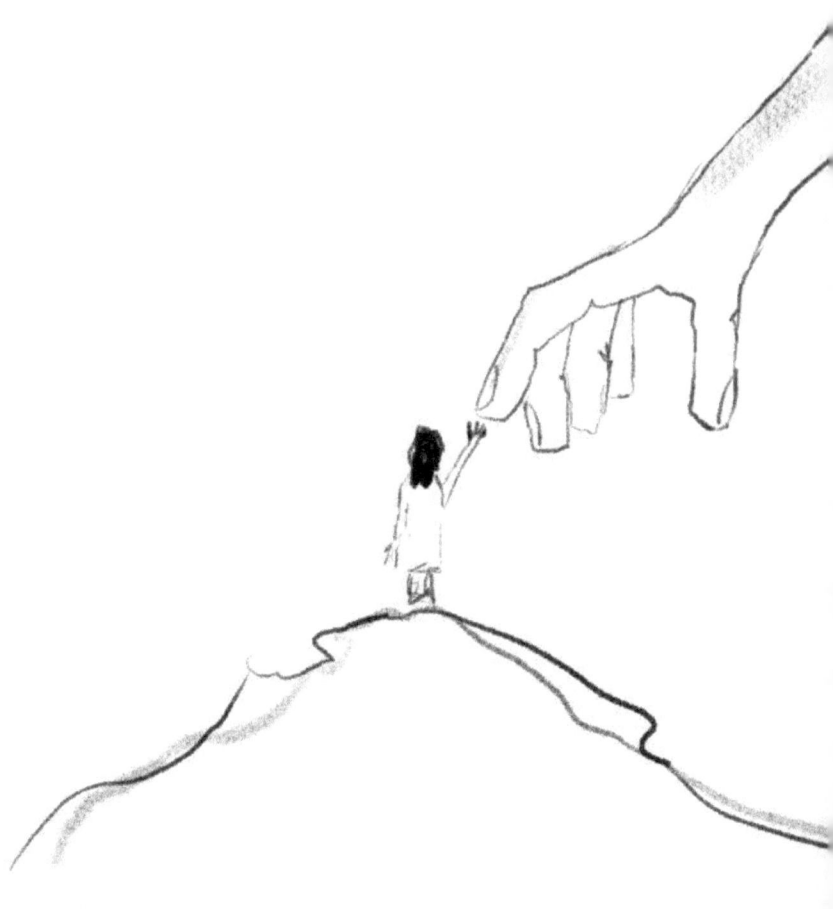

51. WINGS

We have now arrived at the third chapter of our journey. Like a phoenix that has grown its wings, **we are ready to rise and soar.** This is a time to look forward, to envision the future, and to embrace the possibilities for growth and transformation.

This chapter serves as a gentle guide through the transformative process, inviting you to welcome change and plant the seeds of new intentions. As we move forward, you'll learn how to find safety not only in structure and logic, but also in intuition and emotional depth. There is strength in the right hemisphere of the brain—in the Feeler—where softness, imagination, and trust come alive.

By the end of this chapter, you will feel empowered to navigate transformation with confidence. You'll discover essential tools for embracing change, gain a clearer vision of your future self, practice unconditional love, manage your energy more wisely, and dive deeper into your passions and purpose. Together, we'll also explore the concept of "mistakes" and offer you mindset-shifting tools to support your growth.

52. ESSENCE OF TRANSFORMATION

As we journey onward, we arrive at the brink of profound transformation. This chapter invites us to lean into change, to recognize its gifts, and to channel its energy as we grow into the most expansive version of ourselves.

DISCOVERING INNER STRENGTH

True transformation begins within. It invites us to journey inward, to uncover the quiet strength resting deep in our being. You've already looked back on the challenges you've faced—and in doing so, you've witnessed how each experience has shaped you. Every obstacle has been a teacher, every hardship a step toward resilience. And now, this inner strength propels you into what comes next.

SETTING NEW INTENTIONS

Transformation offers a sacred invitation to redefine your path. In the pages ahead, you'll be guided to set fresh intentions—anchored in clarity, purpose, and desire. What goals are calling to you? What dreams have been waiting patiently to come alive?

WELCOMING CHANGE WITH COURAGE

Change can be daunting, but it is also a powerful catalyst for growth. Embrace it with courage and an open heart. Step out of your comfort zone and try new things—whether it's learning a new skill, meeting new people, or exploring unfamiliar places. Each experience broadens your horizons and enriches your life.

BUILDING A SUPPORTIVE COMMUNITY

Surround yourself with a supportive community that encourages your growth and celebrates your successes.

Connect with like-minded individuals who share your vision and values. Share your journey with them—and offer your support in return.

Together, you can create a strong and positive network that uplifts everyone.

NURTURING SELF-LOVE AND COMPASSION

As you transform, remember to nurture self-love and compassion. Be gentle with yourself, honoring both your achievements and your mistakes.

Understand that growth is a process, and it's perfectly okay to stumble along the way. Treat yourself with the same kindness and understanding you would offer to a dear friend.

REFLECTING ON YOUR JOURNEY

Take time to reflect on your journey so far. Look back on the progress you've made, the obstacles you've overcome, and the growth you've experienced.

Celebrate your achievements and let them motivate you to keep moving forward.

Your journey is unique, and every step you take stands as a testament to your strength and determination.

LOOKING TO THE HORIZON

As the phoenix continues to rise, so do your possibilities. Look to the horizon and envision the future you desire.

Embrace the transformation unfolding within you, and trust your ability to navigate the path ahead.

The future is a blank canvas, and you are the artist—ready to paint a life vibrant with meaning, authenticity, and true to your heart.

53. YOUR FUTURE SELF

– Required time: up to you –
– You need: pen –

Read the prompt and freewrite your thoughts.

Write a letter to your future self.

Include all the elements you wish to see in your future life: how and where you want to live, with whom you want to share your life, and how your daily routine will be structured. Go into as much detail as possible—name the main color of your interior design and describe the characteristics of the friends or animals you live with.

*Dear future self, ...*_____

_____

_____

_____

_____

_____

_____

_____

_____

_____

_____

_____

_____

_____

_____

_____

_____

_____

_____

_____

_____

_____

_____

_____

_____

_____

_____

_____

_____

_____

_____

_____

_____

_____

_____

_____

_____

I wish that today, when you look in the mirror, you fall in love with yourself. I hope you realize that the search can finally end because in that reflection, you find the unconditional love you've always sought.

More than that, I wish for you to see that the search was never necessary. The answer has always been within you—tangible yet distant, like the moon and the sun.

—because if you understand that,
then maybe i can too?

54. UNCONDITIONAL LOVE

– Required time: up to you –
– You need: yourself & mirror –

Step 1: Preparation

Find a quiet, comfortable place where you can be alone and undisturbed. Have a mirror nearby—preferably one that shows your entire face clearly. Take a few deep breaths to center yourself and bring your focus fully into the present moment.

Step 2: The Reflection

Stand or sit in front of the mirror and look deeply into your own eyes. Spend a few moments simply observing your reflection without any judgment.

Step 3: Self-Affirmation

Slowly repeat the following affirmation aloud:

"Today, as I gaze into the mirror, I wrap myself gently in a cloak of love. At last, I realize the search has ended—here, in this reflection, lies the boundless, unconditional love I have been seeking all along."

Pause for a moment. Let these words settle deep within you. Feel their profound truth resonate through your being.

Step 4: Reflection and Realization

Continue looking into your eyes and say:

"Even more than that, I wish for you to recognize that you never had to embark on the search from the beginning. The answer has always been within you—steady, silent, and waiting to be embraced."

Step 5: Embracing the Understanding 𓂀𓈖

Now, speak to yourself with compassion and understanding:
"Because if you understand that, then maybe I can too.«

Acknowledge that this exercise is as much about accepting yourself as it is about recognizing the unconditional love within you. The answer has been with you all your life, tangible yet distant, like the moon and the sun.

Reflect on these words and how they apply to your life. Remember that the love and acceptance you seek have always been within you, waiting patiently for you to come home.

Step 6: Closing the Exercise 𓂀𓈖

Take a few more deep breaths, maintaining eye contact with yourself.

End the exercise with gratitude. Thank yourself for taking the time to connect deeply and honestly with your own reflection.

Now, write down any thoughts, feelings, or realizations that came up during the exercise:

_____

_____

_____

_____

_____

_____

_____

_____

Step 7: Daily Practice

Make this exercise a daily practice. Each day, spend a few moments looking into the mirror and reaffirming your unconditional self-love.

Notice how your feelings and perceptions evolve over time, as you become more connected to and accepting of yourself.

≡

55. ENERGY MANAGEMENT

– Required time: 15 min –
– You need: pen & timer –

Reflecting on my journey, I realize how important it became to include activity breaks and prioritize adequate sleep by my mid-forties. My hope for you is that you come to understand this much sooner than I did.

Reflection: take some time to reflect on your own life journey. Consider how you have managed your time and energy so far, especially regarding activity breaks and your sleep habits. How have these influenced your overall well-being and productivity? What changes might help you feel more balanced and energized moving forward?

Up to now, I have managed my time and energy in the following manner: _____

_____

_____

_____

_____

_____

_____

_____

_____

_____

_____

Consideration: think about the significance of incorporating regular activity breaks and prioritizing adequate sleep in your life. Reflect on how your choices in these areas have affected your health, energy levels, and overall well-being. How might making intentional changes improve your daily experience and long-term vitality? _____

_____

_____

_____

_____

_____

_____

_____

_____

Goal Setting: set clear goals for yourself to integrate self-care into your daily life. **Consider specific steps you can take to schedule regular activity breaks and improve your sleep habits.:** _____

_____

_____

_____

_____

_____

_____

_____

_____

_____

_____

_____

_____

_____

_____

_____

Action Plan: develop a concrete action plan to achieve your goals by incorporating your personal needs, schedule, and potential barriers. For example, set a goal to jog every Monday, Wednesday, and Friday at 7:00 AM to improve fitness, while also saving 150 EUR each month by setting up an automatic transfer. Consider obstacles like a lack of morning motivation or unexpected expenses, and plan solutions such as preparing your workout clothes the night before or creating an emergency fund to maintain your savings habit:_____

_____

_____

_____

_____

_____

_____

_____

_____

_____

Reflection: after a week of implementing your action plan, reflect on your progress and return here. Notice any changes you observe and how they are impacting your well-being:

_____

_____

_____

_____

_____

_____

_____

_____

_____

_____

_____

_____

_____

_____

_____

_____

_____

_____

_____

_____

_____

_____

56. WHAT BRINGS ME JOY?

– Required time: 15 min –
– You need: pen & timer –

This exercise invites you to reflect on the sources of joy in your life. Set a timer for 15 minutes and, with a pen in hand, write down 10 things that bring you happiness—whether activities, people, or experiences.

By identifying these elements, you'll gain a clearer understanding of what adds positivity to your life and how you can nurture these sources more often.

1. _____

_____

2. _____

_____

3. _____

_____

4. _____

_____

5. _____

_____

6. _____

_____

7. _____

_____

8. _____

_____

9. _____

_____

10. _____

_____

57. PASSION

I encourage you to **find something in your life that ignites your passion**—something you won't give up on, even during tough times, and into which you will invest your effort so your work can eventually bear fruit like a rich harvest. This might be an art form, such as dance or singing.

Next, **discover a purpose bigger than yourself**, beyond your ego and personal space. Don't lose sight of this greater mission; nurture it so it can grow. Perhaps it's volunteering with an NGO, engaging in social work, or opening your home to strangers through couchsurfing.

Whatever it is, hold on to it firmly. Because only by pursuing a goal that serves others will your life gain true meaning.

58. WHAT'S MY PASSION?

– Required time: ongoing process –
– You need: pen, reflective mind –

If you're unsure what brings passion into your life, take some time to **reflect on past experiences**. Look for patterns—activities that consistently brought you joy. On the next page, **write down ten things you enjoyed doing**, no matter how insignificant they might seem to others. What matters most is your own level of pleasure, so be generous with yourself.

Find a quiet, comfortable place to sit and focus on the drawing provided. As you meditate, gently ask yourself, **"What is my passion?"** Allow your mind to relax and open to the possibilities. Let any thoughts or images that arise flow naturally, without judgment. This process will help you connect with your inner desires and bring clarity to what truly excites and fulfills you.

59. FIND YOUR LIFE PURPOSE

– Required time: maybe even never ending –
– You need: pen, clear mind & your heart full of love –

Here are some exercises to help you discover a larger purpose. As you may notice, much of this has already been explored throughout this book. I offer this summary to empower you to decide whether you'd like to revisit specific exercises here or gently engage with these prompts again.

REFLECTION AND JOURNALING

Find a quiet place to sit and write about your passions, values, and the things that bring you joy. Reflect on what you want to achieve in your life and the legacy you wish to leave behind.

MEDITATION AND MINDFULNESS

Practice regular meditation to clear your mind and cultivate inner peace. Mindfulness exercises help you stay present and explore deeper within yourself.

SELF-ANALYSIS EXERCISES

Answer questions such as, "What would I do if money were no object?", "Which topics move me the most?", and "When do I feel most alive?"

VOLUNTEERING

Engage in volunteer work across different fields to discover what truly matters to you. Volunteering offers fresh perspectives and can help you uncover your true calling.

MENTORS AND ROLE MODELS

Seek out mentors or role models who have discovered a larger purpose in their lives. Learn from their experiences and allow their journeys to inspire your own.

CREATIVE ACTIVITIES

Engage in creative activities like painting, writing, or playing music. These pursuits can help you express yourself more fully and uncover deeper insights into your desires and dreams.

EXPERIENCING NATURE

Spend time in nature to ground yourself and connect with the greater whole. Whether hiking, camping, or simply walking in the park, these moments can be deeply inspiring.

EDUCATION AND COURSES

Attend workshops, courses, or seminars focused on personal development and discovering your life's purpose. These experiences can provide valuable tools and fresh perspectives to guide your journey.

VISUALIZATION

In a visualization exercise, imagine your ideal life in vivid detail. What role do you play within this vision, and how do you contribute to the well-being and happiness of others?

CONVERSATIONS WITH FRIENDS & FAMILY

Discuss your thoughts and feelings with trusted friends and family. Often, others can offer insights you might not have considered.

I
THINK
HARDER.

60. TAKING RESPONSIBILITY

Take responsibility for your own problems, but avoid taking responsibility for your partner's problems, emotions, or actions. Sharing your struggles with your partner can help both of you feel supported, but don't feel obligated to fix their issues.

In my experience, relationships often involve two contrasting personality types: the savior and the victim. Entitlement and poor boundaries tend to be key issues in these dynamics. Both want to feel important — the savior believes they earn affection only by "helping," while the victim believes...

A love declaration from the victim might be:
"Look, dear, this is my problem. You don't need to fix it—just support me while I work through it."

As a victim, don't hold your partner responsible for your problems.

A love declaration from the savior might be:
"Look, you're blaming others for your own problems. It's something you need to deal with yourself."

Remember, sacrifices in a relationship are healthy when done voluntarily, not out of guilt. So ask yourself this question:

Do I act out of obligation/ guilt
or
do I act volunteering?

Keep strong boundaries. Don't be afraid to be hurt, don't be afraid of arguments. Maybe the following sentence helps:

**"I will hurt my partner's emotions
but I can't determine how others feel."**

Whenever two people use their love to escape their individual problems, the relationship is likely unhealthy. Healthy love means acknowledging each other's struggles and supporting one another—not to save, but to empower each other to grow and heal.

61. BOUNDARIES IN A RELATIONSHIPS

– Required time: up to you –
– You need: pen –

In my experience, the following key questions often determine the success of a relationship:

1. How well is one person accepting responsibility?

2. What is the degree of willingness to reject and be rejected by the partner?

Use the next two and a half pages to write about questions 1 and 2—whether in relation to the relationship you are currently in, the last one that ended, or the one you hope to have in the future.

Don't impose any further limitations. Trust your gut and let your thoughts flow freely!

_____

_____

_____

_____

_____

_____

_____

_____

_____

_____

62. MISTAKES

– Required time: 20 minutes –
– You need: pen –

We all make mistakes—and we will continue to make them. It's part of our human nature. Accepting this truth helped me come to terms with myself and with others.

Especially when it comes to men, I used to struggle with how to respond when a man made a mistake. There was a time when I would get really angry. But I learned that men can sense when I am overwhelmed by emotions I can't control. I also realized that if I were determined to disqualify men, I could always find a reason.

So, if you want to be with a man, you can't be too picky. You have to accept him exactly as he is—and make peace with the difference between who he is and who you want him to be. This difference—the "delta"—is the price you pay for the relationship. The size of this delta varies from man to man. Please remember, I am not encouraging "shopping" for men, but it's helpful to recognize that this delta can be huge and difficult to accept—or small and easy to live with. If you have found the man of your dreams, here is a lovely mantra that might help keep the spirit between you both alive:

"I accept you exactly the way you are. Your imperfections are fully part of you. There is nothing in you, I want to change."

Vice versa applicable of course.

After reading the mantra, use this page to **fully express your acceptance of the person currently closest to you** —whether that is a friend, your partner, a beloved animal, or a family member. Address your message directly to this person.

Since space is limited, choose your words thoughtfully and with care. This is not a freewriting exercise; it is an intentional expression of acceptance and presence.

OUT
OF SYSTEM.
- HOW ABOUT YOU?

From THE SKY AND THE SALT, page 240

63. CHANGE OF MIND

– Required time: up to you –
– You need: pen –

The biggest barrier to change is often our own mind and the beliefs we hold. Change itself can be simple and effortless, yet many people cling to their problems because these struggles give them a sense of uniqueness or importance — a kind of attachment to the role of victim. Their problems become part of their identity.

But there is always a way out. Take control of your beliefs. Problems are not permanent states of being. As long as we change the way we think, we will change the way we feel. The greatest challenge is learning how to step out of our own way.

Take control of your life by:

- **taking action**
- **if you do, you will get results**
- **if you don't, you won't**

It's as simple as this: the questions "What went wrong?" or "Why?" are often irrelevant. If you have learned to behave in a certain way, you have created habits — or, in many cases, fears disguised as habits. Be mindful of your habits, as they can quietly erode your quality of life and steal your freedom. Take charge and manage your habits intentionally.

One of the best habits you can cultivate is the habit of feeling happy. Each morning, ask yourself:

"How much fun can I have today?«

Therefore, you need to reach the point where you say:

"I'm fed up thinking about what scares me:"

Shift your perspective—if you constantly look for difficulties, you will always find them. "What can go wrong?" is a question that almost guarantees you'll find something. Instead, ask yourself:

"What works?"

From what I've observed in anxious people, they often build rituals to ward off their fears. Each ritual might bring a small sense of comfort, but in the long run, it only fuels more fear. The more comfort you try to create, the more fear you end up needing.

Since I am in love with freedom, adventure, and joy, I regularly push myself out of my comfort zone. What feels exhausting at first always ends up expanding my mind. For example, when I travel with my backpack, I choose simple rooms—sometimes without a bathroom—and always take cold showers to practice grounding.

Our bodies are not disconnected from our brains. Emotions are active processes—they move and flow within us. You can actually locate where you feel your emotions in your body. It doesn't matter where you feel them, but what you do with them that counts.

For this body exercise, I invite you to close your eyes and take a few deep breaths—in and out. Repeat this as often as feels comfortable. Then, turn your attention inward and notice where your emotions are stored in your body today. Maybe it's your stomach, your chest, your heart, or somewhere entirely different.

Place your awareness gently on that spot.

Can you feel how the emotions move?

Where do they travel—upwards or downwards, to the front or back, left or right?

Gently follow the flow with your hand. It's best if your eyes remain closed.

Now, take control of this movement. **Guide your emotions with your hand**—move them up and down, towards your arms, down your legs. Explore and play with this sensation.

Take a moment to **describe your experience** in a few sentences.

Freestyle—let your words come naturally. Don't overthink it.

_____

_____

_____

_____

_____

_____

_____

_____

_____

_____

_____

_____

_____

_____

_____

As you have experienced, you can influence and guide your emotions. This shows that the quality of your thoughts directly shapes how you feel. When you amplify your emotions with dramatic stories in your mind, the feelings intensify—and when you calm your thoughts, the emotions soften.

If personal freedom is your goal, learning to manage your thoughts is essential.

For the next exercise, **please write down five specific situations where you anticipate needing to practice controlling your thoughts.** For each situation, describe it in one sentence, then briefly explain how you plan to intervene—how you will maintain control of your mind and avoid getting triggered (intervention):

First situation: _____

_____

First intervention:_____

_____

_____

_____

_____

Second situation: _____

_____

Second intervention:_____

_____

_____

_____

_____

_____

Third situation: _____

_____

Third intervention:_____

_____

_____

_____

_____

Forth situation: _____

_____

Forth intervention:_____

_____

_____

_____

_____

Fifth situation: _____

_____

Fifth intervention:_____

_____

_____

_____

_____

_____

_____

64. CHANGING NEUROCHEMISTRY

– Required time: up to you –
– You need: pen –

For this exercise, grab a pen and some colored markers or pencils—get ready to draw.

Think back to a moment when you truly felt good—really step inside that memory. See the scene through your own eyes, hear the sounds around you. Now, make that image bigger, brighter, more colorful. Let the sounds become louder and more vivid.

Now, bring that memory to life on paper. Draw what you see and feel, using colors to express the richness of the moment.

Now, bring your attention to your body and notice where that good feeling begins. Follow its movement—where does it travel inside you? Does it rise, fall, spin, or flow in a certain direction?

Draw a simple outline of your body. Use arrows, colors, or shapes to show where the feeling moves and how it flows within you. Let your drawing capture the energy and movement of that positive emotion.

As a final step, close your eyes again and bring your attention back to that feeling inside your body. Visualize it beginning to spin—slowly at first, then faster and faster, like a washing machine in full motion. Notice how the feeling intensifies and grows stronger with each rotation.

Remember, you can use this simple technique anytime you want to amplify positive emotions and boost your inner energy.

as long as your mind
is solely focused on chasing pleasure
and fleeing pain at all costs,
love will slip through your fingers.

65. GRATITUDE

Gratitude is a vital ingredient in a joyful life. When we cultivate gratitude, our focus shifts—from what we lack to what we already have, from absence to presence. Remember: your focus shapes your reality.

This shift in mindset is a powerful source of energy. Regularly practicing gratitude elevates our overall well-being and awakens positive feelings. It invites us to notice the small wonders that often go unseen and to savor the present moment instead of endlessly chasing external achievements.

In my own daily routine, I make it a habit to name three beautiful moments from my day just before falling asleep. This simple ritual gently guides me into peaceful rest and often brings sweet dreams—some vivid enough to linger in my memory the next morning.

I invite you to practice gratitude right now. Take a moment to write down three things you are grateful for in this very moment—whether it's the gentle sunshine streaming through your window, the sweet strawberry resting on your plate, or even the breath you just took.

Be open. Be present. Let your awareness settle into the simple gifts around you.

To deepen this practice, place a pen and paper beside your bed. **Each night, before you drift to sleep, jot down three things you're grateful for that day.** Carry this ritual forward, night after night, and watch how your heart and mind begin to shift.

*Today, I'm especially thankful for...*_____

_____

_____

_____

_____

_____

_____

_____

_____

_____

_____

_____

_____

_____

_____

_____

DAY BY DAY,
I AM
REALIZING
WHAT
I AM NOT,
AND
I LOVE IT.

66. DAY IMPROVISATION

– Required time: the whole day –
– You need: free time & yourself –

Improvise your day!

Choose a day when you won't plan anything. Spend the day as you decide, spontaneously.

Avoid staying at home!

Here are some simple invitations to sprinkle a little adventure and connection into your day:

♡ Wander through your neighborhood on foot and let yourself get wonderfully lost—no maps, no agenda, just curiosity.

♡ Invite your mother, a friend, or someone you love to a spontaneous lunch—no planning, just show up.

♡ Strike up a conversation with a stranger. Keep smiling and let the exchange surprise you.

♡ Visit a local landmark or attraction you've never been to before—be a tourist in your own town.

♡ Hop on a bus or train without knowing where it's headed. Let the journey unfold like a story.

♡ Take a walk and, at every intersection, only turn right.

♡ Try a cuisine or restaurant you've never experienced.

♡ Spend time in a park or beside a lake, river, or sea—simply watch, listen, and breathe in the calm.

Write down your experiences in freewriting style:

_____

_____

_____

_____

_____

_____

_____

_____

_____

_____

_____

_____

_____

_____

_____

_____

_____

_____

_____

_____

_____

_____

_____

_____

_____

_____

_____

_____

67. BELIEVES

– Required time: up to you –
– You need: markers, paints, pencils & music that inspires reflection –

Unless you believe you can get over it, there is little likelihood that you will be able to do so. As soon as we believe in something, we start searching for ways to prove it's true. Real change can only happen when a person decides that enough is enough.

"I am just not doing this anymore."

A. Reflective Meditation

Find a comfortable position to sit or lie down. Close your eyes and take a few deep breaths to relax. Reflect on the quote, *"I am just not doing this anymore,"* and what it means to you personally. Consider times when you felt stuck or in need of change but lacked the belief in yourself to take the next step.

B. Body Movement Exploration

Stand up and begin to move your body in a way that expresses your feelings about the phrase *"Enough is enough."* Start with gentle stretches to open up and release any tension you may be holding. Let your movements flow naturally—whether it's a deliberate shake to let go of stress or a strong, decisive gesture that signifies determination and strength. You might choose to move to music that inspires empowerment and resolve, allowing each beat to guide you. Focus on how your body feels as you move, and use this time to let go of any negative energy or past obstacles, embracing a sense of renewal and resilience.

C. Artistic Expression

Return to your seated position and take a few deep breaths to center yourself.

On the next page, begin to create an **abstract or representational drawing** using colored pencils. Let your **artwork symbolize the decision to no longer accept what has been holding you back**.

Use colors, shapes, and lines to express empowerment and liberation. Let your drawing reflect your belief in your ability to overcome obstacles and initiate positive change.

Focus on the emotions and insights that surfaced during your reflection. Incorporate elements that embody your inner strength, your clarity, and your vision for an empowered future.

Let this creative expression become a visual affirmation of your commitment to moving forward. Once you've completed your drawing, take a moment to review it and reflect on how it represents your transformation.to your seated position. Take a few deep breaths to center yourself.

D. Reflect and Write

Take a moment to explore how this artistic process has deepened your commitment to overcoming obstacles and continuing on your path of transformation.

Reflect on how creating this piece of art has connected you with the inner truth behind the phrase *"enough is enough"*— and how it has strengthened your belief in your capacity for change.

Consider how the act of expressing your emotions and insights through color, form, and gesture has reinforced your resolve to grow, evolve, and step fully into your power.

Let this reflection be an acknowledgment of your courage —and a quiet celebration of your unfolding journey.

*Engaging in this process has reinforced my belief that...*_____

_____

_____

_____

_____

_____

_____

_____

_____

_____

_____

_____

_____

_____

68. DREAMS COME TRUE

– Required time: up to you –
– You need: pen –

Read the prompt, and freewrite your thoughts.
Use all pages.

Describe a journey you've always dreamed of taking.

*Ever since I can remember, I've wanted to travel to...*_____

_____

_____

_____

_____

_____

_____

_____

_____

_____

_____

_____

_____

_____

_____

_____

_____

_____

_____

_____

_____

_____

_____

_____

_____

_____

_____

_____

_____

_____

_____

_____

_____

_____

_____

_____

_____

_____

_____

_____

_____

69. NEW WORLD

– Required time: up to you –
– You need: pen –

Read the prompt, and free write your thoughts:

INVENT A NEW WORLD WITH ITS OWN RULES AND CHARACTERS.

_____

_____

_____

_____

_____

_____

_____

_____

_____

_____

_____

_____

_____

_____

_____

_____

_____

70. WHAT ARE YOU CELEBRATING TODAY?

– Required time: 10 minutes –
– You need: pen, timer –

In this exercise, set aside 10 minutes to reflect on the positive aspects of your day. **Set a timer, take a pen, and begin listing the moments—big or small—that you're celebrating today.** These might include a personal achievement, a kind word exchanged, a quiet moment of joy, or a simple feeling of contentment. By focusing on what has gone well, you cultivate the habit of appreciation and strengthen your sense of inner well-being. Remember: celebrating the small wins is just as vital as honoring the big ones—because together, they create the fabric of a fulfilled life.

_____

_____

_____

_____

_____

_____

_____

_____

_____

_____

_____

_____

71. HOW CAN I MAKE THE REST OF THE DAY GREAT?

– Required time: 10 minutes –
– You need: pen, timer –

_____

_____

_____

_____

_____

_____

_____

_____

_____

_____

_____

_____

_____

_____

_____

_____

_____

_____

_____

_____

_____

_____

_____

These past two short reflection exercises are designed to support your personal transformation by helping you consciously shape your day and celebrate the progress you're making along the way. By regularly asking yourself what you're celebrating today and how you can make the rest of the day great, you shift your focus toward gratitude and intentional action.

With just a few minutes and a pen, you can clarify your thoughts and take meaningful steps toward growth. These simple practices cultivate mindfulness and a positive mindset, laying the foundation for lasting change over time.

I encourage you to add these two questions to your daily toolkit.

72. THOUGHTS

– Required time: up to you –
– You need: pen –

We all have thoughts—this is simply part of being human, and it's impossible to stop them entirely. Trying to stop thinking would be like asking a dolphin not to swim; it's in our nature. But what we can do is become more aware of the quality and direction of our thoughts. Instead of letting thoughts run wild or overwhelm us, we can start by asking ourselves:

**"How can I use the energy
– aka my thoughts –
for things I truly care about."**

For example, if you notice yourself dwelling on negative scenarios or replaying past mistakes, gently shift your focus toward more constructive thinking. You might ask yourself: *"What can I do today that supports my goals or aligns with my passions?"*

Consider how your thoughts can serve something bigger than yourself — whether it's your community, a cause you believe in, or even your own personal growth. By doing this, you redirect your mental energy toward purposeful action, turning your thoughts into a powerful tool for positive change.

Make a list of 10 things and actions
you want to serve today:

1. _____

_____

2. _____

_____

3. _____

_____

4. _____

_____

5. _____

_____

6. _____

_____

7. _____

_____

8. _____

_____

9. _____

_____

10. _____

_____

73. RISE, PHOENIX

– Required time: up to you –
– You need: pen –

In this final exercise, we will connect with the powerful symbol of the phoenix—a creature that rises from its ashes, transformed and renewed.

Take a moment to reflect on your own journey of transformation. Think once more about the patterns, beliefs, or habits that no longer serve you, and visualize them as the ashes of your past self.

Close your eyes and imagine those ashes being swept away by the wind as you rise from them like a phoenix.

See yourself renewed—stronger, lighter, and free from old limitations. Focus on the vibrant colors, the feeling of weightlessness, and the deep sense of freedom that comes with this new beginning.

Now, on the next page, draw and/or write your vision of the phoenix that represents your new self.

What qualities, strengths, and desires will rise with you as you step into this new chapter of your life? Let your creativity flow—use colors, words, or symbols that resonate with your transformation.

As you complete this exercise, take a few deep breaths and affirm to yourself:

**"I rise renewed.
I carry forward only what serves my highest self.
I am free, I am powerful, I am becoming."**

Welcome the energy of renewal and allow yourself to move forward with confidence, clarity, and purpose—just like the phoenix.

Take a photo of your creation with your smartphone and keep it with you as a reminder of how powerful you are.

CONCLUSION

what now?

The issue with books like this is that, once you reach the end, it can feel final. You might know what to do, yet still feel the same as before. The aim of this book is for you to discover what drives you and who you truly are in this very moment. It doesn't matter what I believe, as I don't have all the answers either. View this book as a starting point, and see the tools I've provided as resources you can always return to.

Of course, there will be moments in your future when you feel sad. Life is unpredictable, and sometimes it can be overwhelming. In fact, just before I started writing this chapter, I found myself in tears. I was exhausted, and it took me a while to realize that I hadn't been taking care of myself —I had been neglecting my own needs. I became complacent, thinking I didn't need to put in any effort. But that's not true: we must always make an effort—and that includes you too.

The difference is that I now feel better equipped to handle the dark times in life. I have a list of things that help me, and as soon as I engage with them, I start to feel better. I hope you have a similar list as well and that you remind yourself of it daily.

Life is a precious gift that we must cherish. To truly live, we must fall in love with it—embracing every moment and finding beauty in the world around us.

Being in love with life means recognizing that we are part of a greater whole and that everything is interconnected. Without love for life, how can we truly love? We can't. So don't let a red traffic light or a long supermarket queue sour your mood and dampen your spirit.

Instead, fall deeply in love with life's highs and lows, surrendering yourself wholly to its boundless possibilities. Only then can you truly love—with an open heart and an open mind.

An open mind listens to the Thinker without letting it dominate; an open heart welcomes the Feeler and allows it to speak. When both are in balance, love flows freely—anchored in clarity, and alive with sensation. This feeling mirrors the exquisite, orgasmic sensation that arises when you make love to your partner.

It is in this realization that you understand you are in the process of BECOMING ME and have learned THE ART OF TRANSFORMATION.

And now you also know why I named my book this way.

Thank you, dear invisible hand,
however you might be called.

Thank you, dear reader and friend,
for being with me, my book, and my ideas until the end.

With love, always.

Yours

Corinna-Rosa Falkenberg

MORE

THE SKY AND THE SALT

ISBN 978–3– 756850273

Divided into three chapters and brought to life with the author's intricate illustrations, 'The Sky and the Salt' takes the reader on a poignant journey through the many facets of inner growth. It is an ode to love.

with my own hands,
i scrubbed the blood from my skin,
crumbling into ashes.
only then did i become the phoenix,
able to spread my wings and soar.

CORINNA-ROSA FALKENBERG

PINKE DELPHINE

PINKE DELPHINE

ISBN 978–3– 756850273

Will you show me your heart?

This is the question young anthropologist Paula must answer after being dangerously bitten by a venomous spider in the Amazon. Weak and vulnerable, she meets a curious girl named Aya in a remote jungle village, who quickly becomes a valuable friend. There, she also encounters the tribal king and, eventually, a wise shaman. In just a few days, Paula comes to realize that the deepest adventures lie not in the terrain we cross, but in the connections we form—connections that can only grow through open hearts. By the end of her stay in the village, Paula embarks on an entirely unexpected journey: a journey into herself. She begins to marvel at a world beyond geography, one that challenges the boundaries imposed by her parents, her peers, and the society she was born into.

"The Little Prince has found his sister in Corinna-Rosa Falkenberg. For the tree of the adult world keeps growing, obscuring our view of what is truly important. A jungle that Falkenberg beautifully illuminates with the adventure of imagination and 'the third eye'—the love." – W.A. Riegerhof, Munich City Writer

Also available as an audiobook everywhere.

DON'T KILL ME, I'M IN LOVE

ISBN 978–3–755727675

Karl and Ada share a deep but irregular love. Karl is married to Maya, with whom he has a young daughter, Lilly, and they live at opposite ends of the country. After years filled with perfect moments, waiting, and hoping, Ada wakes one morning to find that everything has changed. Her once endless willingness to compromise has morphed into raging anger, leading to a radical decision: during a week of solitude in the mountains, she allows her feelings to flow freely, sending unfiltered messages to Karl. In doing so, she shatters the familiar intimacy and beauty of their love, leaving no chance for return.

'Kill Me, I'm in Love' is the chronicle of a catharsis—a liberating break from understanding gray areas, everyday polyamory, and constant deceit. It is a passionate plea for radical clarity in matters of love.

Also available as an audiobook everywhere.

CRAZY FOR LIFE: IN LOVE WITH LIFE

ISBN 978–3–750480285

A book consisting of forty personal stories and observations that take the reader on a journey from Mumbai, through the Tegernseer forest festivals and the Munich district of Lehel, all the way to the Nevada desert for the Burning Man Festival. This collection is a homage to the love of life, crafted with the intention of providing inspiring insights for the reader to contemplate further.

"I consistently felt that I was holding something intensely personal and profound in my hands, something that sticks in the mind and encourages further thought, feeling, and above all, living." – Anneliese Bunk, Spiegel bestseller author.

Also available as an audiobook everywhere.

All illustrations are available as art prints.
www.corinna-rosa.com

SPACE FOR YOUR IMAGE AND WORD

SPACE FOR YOUR IMAGE AND WORD

SPACE FOR YOUR IMAGE AND WORD

SPACE FOR YOUR IMAGE AND WORD

SPACE FOR YOUR IMAGE AND WORD

SPACE FOR YOUR IMAGE AND WORD

SPACE FOR YOUR IMAGE AND WORD

SPACE FOR YOUR IMAGE AND WORD

SPACE FOR YOUR IMAGE AND WORD

SPACE FOR YOUR IMAGE AND WORD

SPACE FOR YOUR IMAGE AND WORD

SPACE FOR YOUR IMAGE AND WORD

SPACE FOR YOUR IMAGE AND WORD

SPACE FOR YOUR IMAGE AND WORD

SPACE FOR YOUR IMAGE AND WORD

Imprint

All rights reserved.

Bibliographic information of the German National Library:

The German National Library records this publication in the German National Bibliography.

Copyright © 2025: Dr. Corinna-Rosa Falkenberg

Typography, typesetting, and cover design: Dr. Corinna-Rosa Falkenberg

Verlag: BoD · Books on Demand GmbH, Überseering 33, 22297 Hamburg, bod@bod.de
Druck: Libri Plureos GmbH, Friedensallee 273, 22763 Hamburg

ISBN: 978-3-7693-5363-1